hamlyn cookery club

Tarts
and pies

hamlyn cookery club

Tarts
and pies

First published in 2000 by Hamlyn
an imprint of Octopus Publishing Group Ltd
2–4 Heron Quays
London E14 4JP

British Library Cataloguing-in-Publication Data
A catalogue record for this book is available from the
British Library.

ISBN 0 600 60074 2

Printed in China

Copy Editor: Heather Thomas
Creative Director: Keith Martin
Design Manager: Bryan Dunn
Designer: Ginny Zeal
Jacket Photography: Sean Myers
Picture Researcher: Rosie Garai
Production Controller: Lisa Moore

Notes

1 Both metric and imperial measurements have been given in all recipes. Use one set of measurements only and not a mixture of both.

2 Standard level spoon measurements are used in all recipes.
1 tablespoon = one 15 ml spoon
1 teaspoon = one 5 ml spoon

3 Eggs should be medium unless otherwise stated. The Department of Health advises that eggs should not be consumed raw. This book may contain dishes made with raw or lightly cooked eggs. It is prudent for more vulnerable people such as pregnant or nursing mothers, the elderly, babies and young children to avoid these dishes. Once prepared, these dishes should be refrigerated and eaten promptly.

4 Milk should be full fat unless otherwise stated.

5 Fresh herbs should be used unless otherwise stated. If unavailable use dried herbs as an alternative but halve the quantities stated.

6 Pepper should be freshly ground black pepper unless otherwise stated.

7 Ovens should be preheated to the specified temperature – if using a fan-assisted oven, follow the manufacturer's instructions for adjusting the time and temperature.

8 Measurements for canned food have been given as a standard metric equivalent.

Contents

Introduction

There is something very satisfying about making your own pastry and it can be made very quickly using a food processor. If time is short then ready made fresh or thawed frozen pasty can be used in most of the recipes in this book. Follow our expert advice below for making your own pastry and you can't go wrong.

THE RIGHT INGREDIENTS
• **Flour:** Most pastry recipes specify plain or wholemeal flour, or even a mixture of the two. Wholemeal flour makes a heavier pastry and absorbs more liquid during mixing. Ideally, the flour should always be sifted to remove any lumps and to introduce more air into the mixture.

• **Fat:** Butter, margarine or lard are usually used. The fat should be at room temperature (unless otherwise specified) to make it easier to rub into the flour. Pastry made with butter is very crisp with a good flavour, whereas margarine gives a more flaky texture. Lard makes the most flaky pastry.

• **Liquid:** Cold water is usually used for mixing the rubbed-in flour and fat to a pliable dough. Never add all the liquid at once – add a little at a time, mixing between each addition until you get the desired texture. The dough should not be too wet nor too dry. Too much water produces a hard, tough pastry, whereas too little water makes the dough tear and crack.

THE GOLDEN RULES FOR SUCCESSFUL PASTRY
• **Stay cool:** The ingredients and your hands should be as cool as possible. If your hands are too warm, the fat may become soft and oily and you will end up with crumbly pastry. Ideally, roll out the dough on some cold marble.

• **Handling the mixture:** When rubbing the fat into the flour, use only your fingertips. As you rub in the fat, lift small pieces into the air above the bowl and then lower your fingertips back down into the flour again. This helps introduce more air and makes a lighter pastry. Don't over-handle the mixture or the dough when you're rolling it out. The less you handle it, the better the pastry will be!

• **The right mix:** When all the fat is thoroughly rubbed into the flour and the mixture looks crumbly, add a little cold water – a tablespoon at a time. The dough should be soft but not sticky nor too dry. If it's too wet, add some flour; too dry, add some more water. Use a round-bladed knife.

• **Resting the dough:** It is best to let the dough rest for 20–30 minutes before rolling it out. This gives the gluten time to react with the water and become more elastic, making the dough easier to roll and less likely to crack. Wrap in clingfilm and chill for 30 minutes to help prevent shrinkage.

• **Rolling out the dough:** Roll out the dough on a lightly floured work surface to help prevent it sticking. Dust the rolling pin with flour beforehand.

• **Cutting out shapes:** To make small pies or tartlets, cut out the pastry with a plain or fluted cutter or cut round an inverted saucer. Dip the cutter in flour first, place it on the dough and press down firmly. Don't twist it.

• **Lining the flan dish:** To transfer the pastry to the prepared dish or plate, place the rolling pin under one end of the rolled-out pastry and roll the pastry around it. Lift the rolling pin over one side of the dish and unroll to cover the dish. Press down gently into position and trim the edges neatly.

BAKING 'BLIND'
Prebaking the pastry case before adding the filling helps to avoid an under-baked base, making it crisper and more appetizing. Line the dish with pastry in the usual way, prick the base with a fork, then crumple up some greaseproof paper or kitchen foil and place it in the centre of the pie. Fill with baking beans and bake in a moderate to hot oven for 10–15 minutes. Remove the paper and beans, and return the pastry case to the oven for 5–10 minutes to dry out the base and lightly colour the edges of the pastry.

Savoury Tarts and Flans

Courgette Flan

The flan can be made up to 24 hours in advance and then kept covered in the refrigerator. Warm through gently in a moderate oven before serving.

175 g (6 oz) plain wholemeal flour
75 g (3 oz) hard vegetable margarine
3 tablespoons water
1 tablespoon vegetable oil
¼ teaspoon salt
Filling:
1 tablespoon vegetable oil
3 courgettes, about 125 g (4 oz), sliced

2 bunches of watercress, stalks removed
2 eggs
150 ml (5 fl oz) soured cream
5 tablespoons milk
salt and pepper

To make the pastry, put the flour and ¼ teaspoon salt in a bowl and rub in the margarine with the fingertips until the mixture resembles fine breadcrumbs. Mix to a firm dough with the water and oil.

Roll out the dough on a lightly floured surface and use to line a 20 cm (8 inch) fluted flan ring. Prick the base with a fork. Place on a baking sheet and then bake in a preheated oven, 200°C (400°F), Gas Mark 6, for 15 minutes to set the pastry without browning.

Meanwhile, prepare the filling. Heat the oil in a frying pan and fry the courgettes quickly on both sides until brown. Remove and drain on kitchen paper.

Add the watercress to the pan and cook for 20 seconds until soft. Remove and chop coarsely. Spread the courgettes and watercress over the base of the flan.

Put the eggs, soured cream and milk in a bowl, season with salt and pepper and whisk together. Pull the centre shelf of the preheated oven out slightly and place the flan case on it, then pour the egg and cream mixture over the courgettes and slide the shelf gently into place.

Bake the flan for about 25 minutes until the filling is set and lightly browned on top. Serve hot or cold.

Serves 4

left: courgette flan
right: cheese and onion oat flan

Mushroom and Onion Quiche

Instead of using mushrooms, you could try a variety of other vegetables. Small broccoli florets, thinly sliced courgettes or fresh peas would work well.

250 g (8 oz) plain flour
125 g (4 oz) butter, diced
2–3 tablespoons cold water
salt
Filling:
15 g (½ oz) butter
1 large onion, thinly sliced
150 ml (¼ pint) milk or single cream
2 eggs
125 g (4 oz) button mushrooms
50 g (2 oz) vegetarian Cheddar
  cheese, grated
salt and pepper

Sift the flour and a pinch of salt into a bowl, then rub in the butter with the fingertips until it resembles fine breadcrumbs. Add enough water to make a firm dough and gently knead together. Roll out the pastry and use to line a 20 cm (8 inch) flan ring set on a baking sheet or a flan dish.

For the filling, melt the butter in a frying pan, then add the onion and cook gently until soft but not brown. Cool slightly and spoon into the pastry case.

Lightly beat together the milk or cream, eggs and salt and pepper to taste. Reserve 3 mushrooms and finely chop the rest. Add to the egg mixture and pour into the pastry case. Thinly slice the reserved mushrooms and scatter over the top. Sprinkle with the cheese.

Bake the quiche in a preheated oven, 200°C (400°F), Gas Mark 6, for 25 minutes until the pastry is cooked and the filling is set.

Serves 4

Cheese and Onion Oat Flan

125 g (4 oz) wholemeal flour
125 g (4 oz) medium oatmeal
125 g (4 oz) margarine
2–3 tablespoons water
salt
Filling:
2 tablespoons oil
2 onions, chopped
2 eggs
150 ml (¼ pint) milk
250 g (8 oz) Cheddar cheese, grated
salt and pepper

Put the flour, oatmeal and a pinch of salt in a mixing bowl and rub in the margarine with the fingertips until the mixture resembles fine breadcrumbs. Add the water and mix to a firm dough.

Turn out onto a floured surface and knead lightly until smooth. Roll out and use to line a 20 cm (8 inch) flan dish. Chill in the refrigerator for 15 minutes.

Meanwhile, make the filling. Heat the oil in a pan, add the onions and fry gently until translucent. Beat the eggs and milk together, and then stir in the cheese, onions, and season with salt and pepper.

Pour into the flan case and bake in a preheated oven, 190°C (375°F), Gas Mark 5, for 35–40 minutes. Serve hot or cold with salad.

Serves 4

Quiche Lorraine

250 g (8 oz) plain flour

½ teaspoon salt

150 g (5 oz) butter or margarine

1–2 tablespoons water

Filling:

250 g (8 oz) thinly sliced bacon, rinded

3 eggs

150 ml (¼ pint) single cream

pepper

Sift the flour and salt into a bowl. Rub in the fat with the fingertips until the mixture resembles fine breadcrumbs. Add the water and mix to a firm dough. Knead lightly until smooth. Wrap in clingfilm or polythene and then chill in the refrigerator for 15–20 minutes.

Roll out the pastry into a round on a lightly floured surface and use to line a 23 cm (9 inch) flan dish or ring. Trim off any excess pastry and prick the base well with a fork. If possible, chill the flan case for a further 20–30 minutes.

Line the pastry case with the bacon rashers and bake on the top shelf of a preheated oven, 200°C (400°F), Gas Mark 6, for 10 minutes.

Lightly whisk together the eggs and cream, adding pepper to taste. Pour over the bacon and return to the oven for 25–30 minutes until set and golden brown. Serve hot.

Serves 6

Individual Asparagus Flans

These flans make a superb summer starter. To cook asparagus, drop it into a pan of boiling salted water and cook for 3–4 minutes until just tender.

375 g (12 oz) plain wholemeal flour

½ teaspoon salt

200 g (7 oz) butter or margarine

4–5 tablespoons cold water

Filling:

1 bunch of asparagus, cooked

300 ml (½ pint) single cream

2 egg yolks

freshly grated nutmeg

salt and pepper

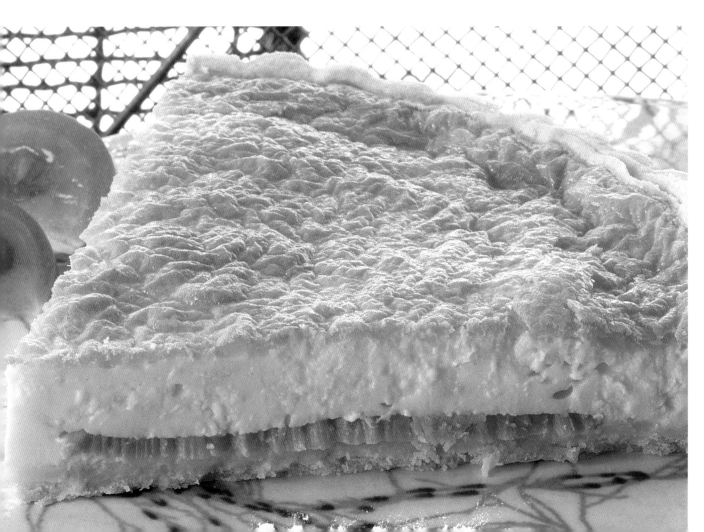

Sift the flour and salt into a bowl, add 175 g (6 oz) of the butter or margarine, and then rub it into the flour with your fingertips until the mixture resembles fine breadcrumbs. Add the water and mix to a dough.

Roll the dough out on a lightly floured board, and then use to line six 10 cm (4 inch) flan tins. Prick the flan bases with a fork and place on a baking sheet. Bake in a preheated oven, 200°C (400°F), Gas Mark 6, for 15–20 minutes until golden brown.

Melt the remaining butter in a pan. Remove the flan cases from the oven and brush with the butter. Reduce the oven temperature to 190°C (375°F), Gas Mark 5.

Trim the asparagus spears and divide between the flans. Whisk the cream and egg yolks together, and then season with salt, pepper and nutmeg. Pour a little of this mixture into each flan case, on top of the asparagus spears.

Return the flans to the oven and bake for about 15 minutes until the filling has set. They should be just firm to the touch and no more.

Serves 6

Onion Tart

250 g (8 oz) plain flour
½ teaspoon salt
50 g (2 oz) butter or margarine
50 g (2 oz) lard
1–2 tablespoons water
Filling:
50 g (2 oz) butter
750 g (1½ lb) onions, sliced
125 g (4 oz) smoked bacon, rinded
   and chopped
25 g (1 oz) plain flour
150 ml (5 fl oz) soured cream
3 eggs, lightly beaten
½ teaspoon salt
½ teaspoon pepper

To make the pastry, sift the flour and salt into a bowl. Rub in the fat with the fingertips until the mixture resembles fine breadcrumbs and then mix to a dough with the water. Use to line a 23 cm (9 inch) flan dish or ring which is placed on a baking sheet.

To make the filling, melt the butter in a pan, add the onions and bacon and fry until soft and golden but not browned. Remove from the heat and then stir in the remaining filling ingredients.

Spoon the onion and bacon mixture into the prepared flan case and smooth the top. Bake in a preheated oven, 200°C (400°F), Gas Mark 6, for about 35–40 minutes until set and golden brown. Serve hot with a salad.

Serves 6

left: quiche Lorraine
above: onion tart

Broccoli and Cheese Flan

125 g (4 oz) wholemeal flour

50 g (2 oz) plain flour, sifted

75 g (3 oz) margarine

50 g (2 oz) mature Cheddar cheese, grated

½ teaspoon dried mixed herbs

1 egg yolk

iced water, to mix

Filling:

250 g (8 oz) broccoli

2 eggs, beaten

150 ml (¼ pint) milk

125 g (4 oz) Cheddar cheese, grated

1 teaspoon dry mustard

salt and pepper

Put the flours in a bowl and rub in the margarine with the fingertips until the mixture resembles fine breadcrumbs. Stir in the cheese and herbs. Make a well in the centre and add the egg yolk and enough water to mix to a firm dough.

Turn out the pastry onto a lightly floured surface and knead lightly until smooth. Roll out and use to line a 20 cm (8 inch) flan dish. Prick the base with a fork, then chill in the refrigerator for 20 minutes.

Fill with foil or greaseproof paper and baking beans and bake 'blind' in a preheated oven, 200°C (400°F), Gas Mark 6, for 10 minutes. Remove the foil or paper and beans, and return to the oven for 5 minutes.

Meanwhile, cook the broccoli in boiling salted water for 5–6 minutes.

Rinse in cold water and then drain thoroughly. Chop coarsely.

Mix the beaten eggs with the milk, three-quarters of the cheese, the mustard, and salt and pepper. Arrange the broccoli in the flan case and pour over the egg mixture. Sprinkle the remaining cheese over the top and return to the oven for 35 minutes until set and golden.

Serves 4

below: broccoli and cheese flan
right: spinach lattice flan

Little Leek Quiches

The leek is a member of the onion family. If they are young, leeks can be chopped finely and used raw in salads. The tougher green tops are best used in long-cook hotpots, stews and soups.

500 g (1 lb) plain flour

375 g (12 oz) butter, diced

2 egg yolks

3 tablespoons water

salt

Filling:

50 g (2 oz) butter

5 large leeks, sliced

1 teaspoon dried oregano

5 eggs

300 ml (½ pint) single cream

1 tablespoon chopped parsley

salt and pepper

For the pastry, sift the flour and a pinch of salt into a mixing bowl. Rub in the butter with the fingertips until the mixture resembles fine breadcrumbs. Bind with the egg yolks and water, and then wrap in some clingfilm and chill in the refrigerator for 20 minutes.

Roll out the pastry and use to line eight 11.5 cm (4½ inch) flan rings placed on baking sheets. Line the pastry cases with foil or greaseproof paper and weigh down with baking beans. Bake 'blind' in a preheated oven, 180°C (350°F), Gas Mark 4, for 15 minutes, then remove the foil or paper and beans and bake for a further 5 minutes.

For the filling, melt the butter in a frying pan, add the leeks and cook gently until softened. Remove from the heat and allow to cool. Sprinkle over the oregano and divide the mixture between the pastry shells.

Beat together the eggs, cream and salt and pepper to taste and pour over the leeks. Sprinkle with the chopped parsley and then bake in the preheated oven for 20 minutes until set and golden.

Makes 8

Spinach Lattice Flan

2 tablespoons oil

1 large onion, chopped

2 garlic cloves, crushed

500 g (1 lb) frozen chopped spinach, thawed and drained

2 eggs

½ teaspoon ground nutmeg

250 g (8 oz) ricotta or curd cheese

50 g (2 oz) Parmesan cheese, grated

salt and pepper

beaten egg, to glaze

Wholemeal shortcrust pastry:

250 g (8 oz) wholemeal flour

125 g (4 oz) plain flour

175 g (6 oz) margarine

3–4 tablespoons iced water

Heat the oil in a pan and fry the onion until softened. Add the garlic and spinach and cook gently for 10 minutes, stirring occasionally. Cool slightly and then beat in the eggs, nutmeg, cheeses, and some salt and pepper to taste.

To make the pastry, put the flours in a mixing bowl and rub in the margarine with the fingertips until the mixture resembles fine breadcrumbs. Add enough water to mix to a firm dough, then turn out onto a lightly floured surface and knead lightly until smooth.

Cut off two-thirds of the pastry, roll out thinly and use to line a 23 cm (9 inch) flan dish, leaving it overlapping the sides.

Spread the filling evenly in the pastry case. Moisten the pastry edge. Roll out the remaining pastry and cut into 5 mm (¼ inch) strips. Arrange in a lattice design over the filling and press the edges to secure.

Brush with beaten egg and bake in a preheated oven, 200°C (400°F), Gas Mark 6, for 45–50 minutes until golden. Serve warm or cold with a crisp mixed salad.

Serves 6

Quiche Paysanne

75 g (3 oz) plain flour, sifted

75 g (3 oz) wholemeal flour

75 g (3 oz) margarine

4–5 tablespoons iced water

salt

Filling:

15 g (½ oz) butter

1 tablespoon oil

4 rashers of bacon, rinded and
   chopped

1 large onion, chopped

2 potatoes, sliced

2 eggs

150 ml (¼ pint) double cream

1 tablespoon each chopped parsley
   and chives

½ red pepper, cored, deseeded and
   chopped (optional)

75 g (3 oz) Cheddar cheese

salt and pepper

Place the flours and a pinch of salt in a bowl and rub in the margarine with the fingertips until the mixture resembles fine breadcrumbs. Add enough water to mix to a firm dough.

Turn out onto a lightly floured surface and knead lightly. Roll out and use to line a 20 cm (8 inch) flan ring on a baking sheet. Prick all over with a fork and then chill in the refrigerator for 30 minutes.

Fill with foil or greaseproof paper and baking beans and bake 'blind' in a preheated oven, 190°C (375°F), Gas Mark 5, for 12–15 minutes until set. Remove the foil or paper and beans and then return to the oven for 5 minutes.

Heat the butter and oil in a pan, add the bacon and cook until lightly browned. Remove and drain on kitchen paper. Add the onion and potatoes to the pan and cook for 12–15 minutes until browned. Drain on kitchen paper.

Beat the eggs and cream together, stir in the herbs and season well with salt and pepper.

Spoon the potatoes, onion and bacon into the flan case and then sprinkle over the red pepper, if using. Pour over the egg mixture and sprinkle with the Cheddar. Return the quiche to the oven for 20–25 minutes until well risen and golden brown. Serve hot or cold.

Serves 6

Watercress Flan

175 g (6 oz) wholemeal flour

75 g (3 oz) margarine

2 tablespoons grated Parmesan
   cheese

1 egg yolk

iced water, to mix

salt

sprigs of watercress, to garnish

Filling:

25 g (1 oz) butter

1 bunch of spring onions, chopped

1 bunch of watercress, finely chopped

3 eggs

150 ml (5 fl oz) soured cream

125 g (4 oz) Cheddar cheese, grated

salt and pepper

Put the flour and a pinch of salt in a bowl and rub in the fat with the fingertips until the mixture resembles fine breadcrumbs. Stir in the Parmesan and egg yolk and then add enough iced water to make a firm dough.

Turn out onto a lightly floured surface and knead lightly. Roll out and use to line a 20 cm (8 inch) flan ring placed on a baking sheet. Prick all over with a fork and chill in the refrigerator for 30 minutes.

Fill with foil or greaseproof paper and baking beans and bake 'blind' in a preheated oven, 190°C (375°F), Gas Mark 5, for 12–15 minutes. Remove the foil or paper and beans and return to the oven for 5 minutes.

Melt the butter in a pan, add the spring onions and cook for 5 minutes. Stir in the watercress and cook gently for 2 minutes until soft.

Beat the eggs and soured cream, stir in the cheese and season with salt and pepper. Spoon the spring onions and watercress into the flan case, pour over the egg mixture and bake for 20–25 minutes until golden. Serve hot or cold, garnished with sprigs of watercress.

Serves 4–6

Quiche Provençal

250 g (8 oz) plain flour
75 g (3 oz) butter
25 g (1 oz) lard
1 egg yolk
iced water, to mix
salt
Filling:
25 g (1 oz) butter
1 onion, sliced
1 garlic clove, crushed
50 g (2 oz) button mushrooms, sliced
1 courgette, chopped
2 large tomatoes, skinned and
   chopped
few basil leaves, chopped
½ teaspoon dried mixed herbs
2 eggs
150 ml (¼ pint) single cream
50 g (2 oz) Cheddar cheese, grated
25 g (1 oz) Gruyère cheese, sliced
salt and pepper

Sift the flour and a pinch of salt into a bowl and rub in the fats with the fingertips until the mixture resembles fine breadcrumbs. Stir in the egg yolk and enough water to make a firm dough.

Turn out onto a lightly floured surface and knead lightly. Roll out and use to line a 23 cm (9 inch) flan ring placed on a baking sheet. Prick all over with a fork and chill in the refrigerator for 30 minutes.

Line with foil or greaseproof paper and baking beans and bake 'blind' in a preheated oven, 190°C (375°F), Gas Mark 5, for 12–15 minutes until set. Remove the foil or paper and beans and return to the oven for 5 minutes.

Melt the butter in a pan, add the onion and garlic and cook gently for 5 minutes. Add the vegetables and herbs, and season well with salt and pepper. Cook over a low heat for 10 minutes.

Beat the eggs and cream together and stir in the grated cheese. Spoon the tomato mixture into the flan case, pour over the egg mixture and carefully arrange the cheese slices on top. Bake in the preheated oven for 25–30 minutes until set. Serve hot or cold.

Serves 6

left: quiche paysanne
above: *quiche Provençal*

Aubergine, Tomato and Mozzarella Flan

1 quantity Shortcrust Pastry
  (see page 94)
5 tablespoons olive oil
1 large aubergine, sliced
4 tomatoes, skinned and sliced
175 g (6 oz) mozzarella cheese, sliced
2 tablespoons chopped basil
¼ teaspoon grated nutmeg
1 egg, beaten
150 ml (¼ pint) passata
salt and pepper
basil leaves, to garnish

Roll out the pastry and use to line a 23 cm (9 inch) fluted flan tin. Fill with foil or greaseproof paper and baking beans and bake 'blind' in a preheated oven, 200°C (400°F), Gas Mark 6, for 15 minutes. Raise the oven temperature to 230°C (450°F), Gas Mark 8.

Brush a baking sheet with some of the oil and arrange the aubergine slices on the sheet in a single layer. Brush the slices with the remaining oil and then sprinkle with salt and pepper. Bake for 25–30 minutes, turning once, until golden brown and soft. Remove from the oven and reduce the temperature to 190°C (375°F), Gas Mark 5.

Arrange overlapping slices of aubergine, tomato and mozzarella in the pastry case and sprinkle with the basil and nutmeg. Beat together the egg and passata and pour over the filling. Bake in the preheated oven for 45 minutes until set. Garnish with basil leaves and serve.

Serves 4–6

Danish Quiche

1 quantity Shortcrust Pastry
  (see page 94)
50 g (2 oz) Danish Blue cheese,
  crumbled
125 g (4 oz) Edam cheese, diced
25 g (1 oz) butter, softened
2 eggs, lightly beaten
450 ml (¾ pint) milk
pinch of cayenne pepper
2 tablespoons chopped spring onions
pepper

Roll out the pastry on a lightly floured surface and use to line a 20 cm (8 inch) flan tin. Fill with foil or greaseproof paper and baking beans, and then bake 'blind' in a preheated oven, 200°C (400°F), Gas Mark 6, for 15 minutes. Remove and lower the oven temperature to 190°C (375°F), Gas Mark 5.

Blend together the cheeses and butter with a fork. Add the eggs, and mix in the milk, seasoning and spring onions.

Pour the mixture into the pastry case and bake in the preheated oven for 20–25 minutes until golden brown and set. Serve hot or cold.

Serves 4

Carrot and Cumin Quiche

175 g (6 oz) plain flour
75 g (3 oz) margarine
2 tablespoons cold water
salt
Filling:
175 g (6 oz) cooked carrots
425 g (14 oz) can butter beans,
  drained
¾ teaspoon ground cumin
3 eggs
125 g (4 oz) Cheddar cheese, grated

Sift the flour and a pinch of salt into a bowl. Cut the margarine into small pieces and rub into the flour with the fingertips until the mixture resembles fine breadcrumbs. Add enough water to mix to a dough.

Roll out the pastry and use to line a 20 cm (8 inch) flan dish or ring, placed on a baking sheet.

To make the filling, blend the carrots, butter beans, cumin and eggs in a blender or food processor. Pour half of the mixture into the flan case, sprinkle with half of the cheese, cover with the remaining carrot and bean mixture and top with the remaining cheese. Bake in a preheated oven, 200°C (400°F), Gas Mark 6, for 40 minutes.

Serves 4

right: aubergine, tomato and mozzarella flan, Danish quiche

Rich Broccoli and Cream Cheese Flan

1 quantity Wholemeal Shortcrust
   Pastry (see page 95)
200 g (7 oz) broccoli florets
150 g (5 oz) cream cheese with garlic
   and herbs
4 eggs
150 ml (¼ pint) milk
4 spring onions, finely chopped
salt and pepper

Roll out the pastry on a lightly floured board and then use to line a 20 cm (8 inch) fluted flan ring set on a baking sheet. Fill with foil or greaseproof paper and baking beans and bake 'blind' in a preheated oven, 200°C (400°F), Gas Mark 6, for 15 minutes.

Remove from the oven and lower the oven temperature to 190°C (375°F), Gas Mark 5.

Blanch the broccoli in boiling water for 3–5 minutes. Drain well and arrange in the pastry case. Beat together the cream cheese, eggs and milk. Season well with salt and pepper and add the spring onions. Pour into the pastry case.

Bake in the preheated oven for 35–40 minutes until the filling is set and golden brown. Serve the flan hot or cold.

Serves 4

Leek Flans

These delicious flans make superb summer starters. Alternatively, you could make them a feature of a summer picnic basket – they're much more impressive than a pile of sandwiches!

175 g (6 oz) wholemeal or plain flour
75 g (3 oz) butter
2–3 tablespoons cold water
Filling:
2 leeks, halved and sliced
1 celery stick, sliced
25 g (1 oz) butter
125 g (4 oz) Danish Bolina cheese
2 eggs, beaten
150 ml (¼ pint) milk
¼ teaspoon grated nutmeg
15 g (½ oz) flaked almonds (optional)
salt and pepper

Sift the flour into a bowl and rub in the butter with the fingertips until the mixture resembles fine breadcrumbs. Add enough water to mix to a stiff dough.

Roll out the pastry on a lightly floured board and then use to line 4 individual flan tins. Fill with foil or greaseproof paper and baking beans and bake 'blind' in a preheated oven, 200°C (400°F), Gas

Mark 6, for 10 minutes, removing the baking beans and foil or greaseproof paper after 7 minutes. Reduce the oven temperature to 190°C (375°F), Gas Mark 5.

Cook the leeks and celery in the butter in a covered pan over a low heat for 5–7 minutes until softened.

Crumble the cheese into a bowl, beat to soften, and then work in the eggs, a little at a time, to make a smooth mixture. Stir in the milk, seasoning and nutmeg.

Divide the cooked vegetables between the flan cases, pour the cheese mixture over them and scatter with almonds, if using. Bake in the preheated oven for 20–25 minutes until set and golden brown.

Serves 4

Dolcelatte and Almond Tart

250 g (8 oz) puff pastry, thawed if frozen
1 egg, beaten
3 tablespoons ground almonds
150 g (5 oz) dolcelatte cheese, diced
3 tablespoons single cream
3 tablespoons flaked almonds
pepper

Roll out the puff pastry to a 25 cm (10 inch) square and trim the edges with a sharp knife. Lift carefully onto a lightly oiled baking sheet.

Using a sharp knife, make two 'L'-shaped cuts in the pastry, in opposite corners, about 2.5 cm (1 inch) from the outer edges. Stop just short of joining the cuts into a square.

Moisten the edges of the pastry with beaten egg. Lift one cut corner and draw it to the opposite side. Lift the other cut corner across to the opposite side, forming a square with raised edges.

Prick the base of the pastry square with a fork, then sprinkle with the ground almonds. Arrange the diced cheese on top, keeping it away from the pastry edges.

Sprinkle with pepper, then drizzle the cream over and scatter with the flaked almonds. Glaze the pastry edges with some beaten egg.

Bake in a preheated oven, 220°C (425°F), Gas Mark 7, for 15–20 minutes until the pastry is cooked and crisp and the filling is well-risen and golden brown. Serve hot.

Serves 4–6

left: rich broccoli and cream cheese flan
below: dolcelatte and almond tart

Purée the tofu in a food processor and stir in the soy sauce and season with salt and pepper. Stir the tofu into the vegetables and then spoon into the pastry case. Sprinkle with sesame seeds and bake in the preheated oven for 20–25 minutes.

Serves 4–6

Red and Yellow Pepper Tart

1 quantity Shortcrust Pastry
  (see page 94)
1 large red pepper, cored, deseeded
  and sliced
1 large yellow pepper, cored,
  deseeded and sliced
1 small onion, thinly sliced
2 garlic cloves, crushed
2 tablespoons olive oil
4 tablespoons dry white wine or stock
2 eggs
2 egg yolks
150 ml (¼ pint) single cream
10 black olives, pitted
salt and pepper

Roll out the pastry on a lightly floured board and then use to line a 23 cm (9 inch) fluted flan tin. Fill with foil or greaseproof paper and baking beans and bake 'blind' in a preheated oven, 200°C (400°F), Gas Mark 6, for 15 minutes. Remove the pastry case and then reduce the oven temperature to 190°C (375°F), Gas Mark 5.

Spicy Tofu and Bean Flan

200 g (7 oz) plain flour
100 g (3½ oz) butter or margarine
125 g (4 oz) frozen chopped spinach,
  thawed and well drained
1 tablespoon sunflower oil
1 small onion, chopped
1 large red pepper, cored, deseeded
  and diced
½ teaspoon chilli powder
200 g (7 oz) can red kidney beans,
  drained and rinsed
300 g (10 oz) packet silken tofu
1 teaspoon light soy sauce
2 tablespoons sesame seeds
salt and pepper

Sift the flour into a bowl and rub in the butter or margarine evenly with the fingertips until the mixture resembles fine breadcrumbs. Stir in the chopped spinach and then mix to a fairly soft dough.

Roll out the pastry on a lightly floured board and then use to line a 23 cm (9 inch) fluted flan tin. Prick the base with a fork.

Fill with foil or greaseproof paper and baking beans and bake 'blind' in a preheated oven, 200°C (400°F), Gas Mark 6, for 15 minutes. Remove and reduce the oven temperature to 190°C (375°F), Gas Mark 5.

Heat the oil and fry the onion and red pepper for 4–5 minutes to soften. Stir in the chilli powder and kidney beans.

Meanwhile, cook the peppers, onion and garlic in the olive oil for 3–4 minutes, stirring. Add the wine or stock and cook over a low heat until the vegetables are softened.

Beat the eggs and egg yolks together, then add the cream and season with salt and pepper. Spread the pepper mixture in the pastry case with the olives and pour in the egg mixture.

Bake the tart in the preheated oven for about 30–35 minutes until the filling is golden brown and set. Serve hot or cold.

Serves 4–6

left: spicy tofu and bean flan
below: fennel and camembert tart

Fennel and Camembert Tart

1 quantity Rich Shortcrust Pastry
 (see page 94)
1 tablespoon olive oil
1 small fennel bulb, finely chopped
150 g (5 oz) camembert cheese, diced
2 tablespoons chopped parsley
2 tomatoes, skinned and diced
1 egg, beaten
1 egg yolk
150 ml (¼ pint) crème fraîche
salt and pepper

Roll out the pastry on a lightly floured surface and use to line a 23 cm (9 inch) fluted flan tin. Fill with foil or greaseproof paper and baking beans and bake 'blind' in a preheated oven, 200°C (400°F), Gas Mark 6, for 15 minutes. Remove the pastry case and reduce the oven temperature to 180°C (350°F), Gas Mark 4.

Heat the oil and gently fry the fennel until soft. Spoon into the pastry case with the cheese, parsley and tomatoes.

Beat together the egg and egg yolk, crème fraîche and seasonings, then pour over the fennel filling. Bake in the preheated oven for 25–30 minutes until set and golden brown. Serve hot or cold.

Serves 4-6

Variation: For a celery and brie tart, use 175 g (6 oz) celery, thinly sliced, instead of the fennel, and substitute brie for the camembert cheese. Bake as described in the recipe above.

Cheese and Onion Rice Tart

1 quantity Rich Shortcrust Pastry
  (see page 94)
25 g (1 oz) butter
1 small leek, thinly sliced
1 garlic clove, crushed
250 g (8 oz) short-grain rice
1 teaspoon turmeric
600 ml (1 pint) chicken stock
3 spring onions, chopped
finely grated rind of 1 lemon
2 tablespoons chopped parsley
1 egg, beaten
75 g (3 oz) cream cheese
50 g (2 oz) mozzarella cheese, grated
  or chopped
50 g (2 oz) grated Parmesan cheese
salt and pepper

Roll out the pastry on a lightly floured board and use to line a 25 cm (10 inch) fluted flan tin. Fill with foil or greaseproof paper and baking beans and then bake 'blind' in a preheated oven, 200°C (400°F), Gas Mark 6, for 15 minutes. Remove the pastry case and reduce the oven temperature to 190°C (375°F), Gas Mark 5.

Melt the butter in a pan and gently fry the leek until soft. Stir in the garlic, rice, turmeric and stock. Cover and simmer gently until the rice is tender and the liquid has been absorbed. Add the spring onions, lemon rind, parsley and seasonings. Beat together the egg and cream cheese and stir into the rice.

Spread the rice mixture in the pastry case and then sprinkle the mozzarella and Parmesan in lines over the top. Bake in the preheated oven for 25–30 minutes or until golden brown and bubbling. Serve hot or cold.

Serves 6

Oyster Mushroom and Parmesan Tart

375 g (12 oz) puff pastry, thawed if
  frozen
25 g (1 oz) butter
2 shallots, finely chopped
125 g (4 oz) oyster mushrooms, sliced
3 tablespoons chopped coriander
3 eggs, beaten
150 ml (¼ pint) double cream
4 tablespoons grated Parmesan
  cheese
salt and pepper

Roll out the pastry on a lightly floured board and then use to line a 23 cm (9 inch) fluted flan tin. Fill with foil or greaseproof paper and baking beans and bake 'blind' in a preheated oven, 220°C (425°F), Gas Mark 7, for 5 minutes. Remove the flan from the oven and reduce the temperature to 180°C (350°F), Gas Mark 4.

Melt the butter and fry the shallots for 3–4 minutes. Add the mushrooms and cook for 2–3 minutes until soft. Spoon into the pastry case and sprinkle with coriander.

Beat together the eggs, cream and season with salt and pepper, and pour into the pastry case. Sprinkle with the Parmesan. Bake in the preheated oven for 20–25 minutes until golden brown.

Serves 4–6

Tomato Tart

1 quantity Shortcrust Pastry
  (see page 94)
750 g (1½ lb) tomatoes
15 g (½ oz) butter
1 large onion, sliced
½ small red chilli, deseeded and
  sliced
1 garlic clove, crushed
salt and pepper
onion rings, to garnish

Roll out the pastry on a lightly floured board and then use to line a 22 cm (8½ inch) flan tin. Fill with foil or greaseproof paper and

left: cheese and onion rice tart
below: tomato tart

baking beans and then bake 'blind' in a preheated oven, 200°C (400°F), Gas Mark 6, for 15 minutes. Remove the pastry case and reduce the oven temperature to 190°C (375°F), Gas Mark 5.

Skin and roughly chop 500 g (1 lb) of the tomatoes. Melt the butter and fry the onion, chilli and garlic for 1 minute. Add the chopped tomatoes and season to taste. Cover and simmer for about 30 minutes until the tomatoes have formed a purée.

Pour the tomato purée into the pastry case. Thinly slice the remaining tomatoes and arrange them over the purée, together with the onion rings. Bake in the preheated oven for 25–30 minutes. Serve hot or cold.

Serves 4

Ricotta and Dill Wholemeal Flan

Ricotta is a soft Italian cheese. If it is unobtainable, you can substitute curd cheese or sieved cottage cheese.

75 g (3 oz) wholemeal flour
75 g (3 oz) self-raising flour, sifted
75 g (3 oz) white cooking fat or lard
2–3 tablespoons water
Filling:
250 g (8 oz) ricotta cheese
1 tablespoon chopped dill
2 eggs, beaten
150 ml (¼ pint) single cream
salt and pepper

To make the pastry, mix together the wholemeal flour and self-raising flour. Rub in the fat with the fingertips until the mixture resembles fine breadcrumbs. Stir in enough water to mix to a soft dough. Cover and chill the pastry in the refrigerator for 30 minutes.

In a bowl, mix together the ricotta, dill, beaten eggs, cream, salt and pepper for the filling.

Roll out the pastry and use to line a 20 cm (8 inch) flan dish. Pour in the filling and bake in a preheated oven, 200°C (400°F), Gas Mark 6, for 20 minutes, then reduce the heat to 180°C (350°F), Gas Mark 4, for a further 20 minutes. Serve cold.

Serves 6

Lambs' Kidneys in Pastry Nests

250 g (8 oz) Shortcrust Pastry
  (see page 94)
40 g (1½ oz) butter
1 onion, finely chopped
1 garlic clove, crushed
6 lambs' kidneys, skinned, cored and
  thinly sliced
15 g (½ oz) flour
150 ml (¼ pint) white wine
150 ml (¼ pint) stock
50 g (2 oz) button mushrooms, sliced
1 tablespoon chopped parsley
2 tomatoes, skinned, deseeded and
  diced
salt and pepper
sprigs of parsley, to garnish

To make the pastry nests, roll out the pastry and use to line 6 foil containers (or ramekin dishes), each 6 cm (2½ inches) in diameter and 2.5 cm (1 inch) deep.

Line the pastry cases with foil or greaseproof paper, then fill them with baking beans. Bake 'blind' in a preheated oven, 190°C (375°F), Gas Mark 5, for 10 minutes. Remove the foil or paper with the beans, and return the pastry cases to the oven for 6–10 minutes until light golden. Allow to cool, then unmould.

To make the filling, melt the butter and add the onion and garlic. Cook gently until pale golden in colour. Add the kidneys to the pan, raise the heat and then fry, stirring, for 2–3 minutes.

Remove from the heat and stir in the flour, then add the wine, stock, mushrooms and parsley. Return the pan to the heat and simmer for 8–10 minutes. Add the tomatoes and season with salt and pepper, just allowing the tomatoes to warm through without breaking up.

Warm the pastry cases through and fill with the kidney mixture. Garnish with sprigs of parsley.

Serves 6

Variation: For a less expensive dish, gently poach some smoked haddock and a little cod in milk. Reserve the cooking liquid, and bone and flake the fish. Make a thick white sauce with the cooking liquid, then gently fold in the flaked fish. Fill the nests, sprinkle with a little grated Cheddar cheese, and cook in a moderate oven for 10–15 minutes before serving

Sausage Slice

1 tablespoon oil
1 small onion, chopped
500 g (1 lb) sausagemeat
1 teaspoon dried mixed herbs
1 egg, beaten
400 g (13 oz) puff pastry, thawed if frozen
1 small cooking apple, peeled, cored and sliced
salt and pepper

Heat the oil in a small frying pan and fry the onion until soft. Tip into a bowl, cool slightly, and then add the sausagemeat with the herbs. Season with salt and pepper and stir in half of the beaten egg.

Roll out three-quarters of the pastry to a 25 cm (10 inch) square and place on a greased baking sheet. Spread the sausagemeat mixture over the pastry to within 1 cm (½ inch) of the edge. Arrange the sliced apple on top. Dampen the edges of the pastry with water.

Roll out the remaining pastry. Cut into 1 cm (½ inch) wide strips and make a woven trellis over the top of the apples. Brush with the remaining beaten egg and chill in the refrigerator for 30 minutes.

Bake in a preheated oven, 220°C (425°F), Gas Mark 7, for 15 minutes. Reduce the oven temperature to 180°C (350°F), Gas Mark 4, and cook for a further 15–30 minutes.

Serves 6

Jellied Chicken and Herb Flan

1 quantity Rich Shortcrust Pastry (see page 94)
3 rashers of streaky bacon, rinded and diced
50 g (2 oz) button mushrooms, sliced
1 chicken stock cube
2 teaspoons powdered gelatine
150 ml (¼ pint) dry white wine
250 g (8 oz) cooked chicken, diced
2 tablespoons chopped mixed herbs

Roll out the pastry on a lightly floured board and use to line a 23 cm (9 inch) plain flan tin. Cut the trimmings into long thin strips and twist 2 together. Moisten the pastry rim with water and press the twist around the edge to decorate.

Fill with foil or greaseproof paper and baking beans and bake 'blind' in a preheated oven, 200°C (400°F), Gas Mark 6, for 15 minutes. Remove the foil or paper and baking beans and bake for a further 5–10 minutes until the pastry is cooked. Cool.

Fry the bacon without fat until lightly browned, then stir in the mushrooms and cook until soft. Remove from the heat and cool.

Dissolve the stock cube in 150 ml (¼ pint) boiling water and stir in the gelatine until dissolved. Add the wine. Allow to cool but not to set.

Fill the pastry case with the chicken, bacon, mushrooms, herbs and seasoning. Pour in the gelatine mixture when it is on the point of setting. Chill in the refrigerator for at least 1 hour until set. Serve cold.

Serves 4–6

Variation: For Chicken and Celery Barquettes, replace the mushrooms with diced celery. Roll out the pastry thinly and use to line 20–24 individual barquette (boat-shaped) tins or small fluted tartlet tins. Prick the bases and bake 'blind' as above. Cool, fill and chill until set.

left: lambs' kidneys in pastry nests

West Country Flan

1 quantity Shortcrust Pastry
  (see page 94)
8 rashers of smoked streaky bacon,
  rinded and chopped
50 g (2 oz) butter or margarine
750 g (1½ lb) leeks, sliced
25 g (1 oz) plain flour
300 ml (½ pint) dry cider
125 g (4 oz) mature Cheddar cheese,
  grated
3 tablespoons double cream
salt and pepper

Roll out the pastry on a lightly floured board and use to line a deep 23 cm (9 inch) flan tin. Fill with foil or greaseproof paper and baking beans and then bake 'blind' in a preheated oven, 200°C (400°F), Gas Mark 6, for 15 minutes. Remove the pastry case from the oven and reduce the oven temperature to 190°C (375°F), Gas Mark 5.

Fry the bacon without fat until lightly browned. Stir in half of the butter, add the leeks and continue to cook, stirring occasionally, until the leeks are soft.

Melt the remaining butter in a saucepan and stir in the flour. Cook, stirring, for 1 minute, and then gradually stir in the cider. Cook over a medium heat, stirring, until thickened and smooth.

Remove from the heat and stir in the cheese, cream and seasonings. Add to the bacon and leeks, and

then spoon into the pastry case. Bake in the preheated oven for 30–35 minutes until the filling is set and golden brown. Serve hot.

Serves 4–6

Curried Chicken Tartlets

1 quantity Shortcrust Pastry
  (see page 94)
2 teaspoons curry powder
2 tablespoons lemon juice
375 g (12 oz) cold cooked chicken,
  skinned and cut into thin strips
125 g (4 oz) walnuts, roughly
  chopped
125–150 ml (4–5 fl oz) mayonnaise
salt and pepper
2 tablespoons finely chopped parsley

Divide the pastry into 4 pieces. Roll out each piece on a lightly floured surface and use to line four 11.5 cm (4½ inch) tartlet tins. Fill with foil or greaseproof paper and baking beans and bake 'blind' in a preheated oven, 200°C (400°F), Gas Mark 6, for 15 minutes. Remove and cool.

Stir the curry powder, lemon juice, chicken and walnuts into the mayonnaise, and season with salt and pepper to taste. Spoon into the cold pastry cases and smooth the surface. Sprinkle with the chopped parsley. Serve cold.

Serves 4

Chicken and Pepper Tart

1 quantity Shortcrust Pastry
(see page 94)
15 g (½ oz) butter
1 onion, sliced
1 garlic clove, crushed
500 g (1 lb) cold cooked chicken,
skinned and diced
1 red pepper, cored, deseeded and
sliced
1 green pepper, cored, deseeded and
sliced
1 tablespoon tomato purée
1 egg, lightly beaten
125 ml (4 fl oz) double cream
½ teaspoon dried thyme
1 tablespoon finely chopped parsley
salt and pepper

Roll out the pastry and use to line a
23 cm (9 inch) flan tin. Fill with foil
or greaseproof paper and baking
beans and bake 'blind' in a
preheated oven, 200°C (400°F), Gas
Mark 6, for 15 minutes. Remove the
flan and reduce the temperature to
190°C (375°F), Gas Mark 5.

Melt the butter and fry the onion
and garlic. Add the chicken and cook
for 2 minutes. Add the peppers, fry
briefly and stir in the tomato purée.

Beat together the egg, cream,
herbs and seasoning. Stir in the
chicken mixture, and spoon into
the pastry case. Bake in the oven for
30–35 minutes until set.

Serves 4–6

Salami and Tomato Flan

1 quantity Wholemeal Shortcrust
Pastry (see page 95) with
1 tablespoon poppy seeds added
3 tablespoons wholemeal
breadcrumbs
1 tablespoon chopped rosemary
175 g (6 oz) salami, thinly sliced and
cut into strips
2 tomatoes, sliced into wedges
2 eggs, beaten
150 ml (¼ pint) milk
½ teaspoon chilli sauce
¼ teaspoon garlic salt

Roll out the pastry on a lightly
floured board and use to line a
23 cm (9 inch) fluted flan tin. Fill
with foil or greaseproof paper and
baking beans and bake 'blind' in a
preheated oven, 200°C (400°F), Gas
Mark 6, for 15 minutes. Remove the
pastry case and then reduce the
oven temperature to 190°C (375°F),
Gas Mark 5.

Sprinkle the breadcrumbs and
rosemary over the base of the pastry
case. Arrange the strips of salami
and tomato wedges on top.

Beat together the eggs, milk,
chilli sauce and garlic salt. Pour into
the pastry case, then bake in the
preheated oven for 30–35 minutes
or until set and golden.

Serves 4–6

left: West Country flan
below: salami and tomato flan

Bacon, Tomato and Cheese Flan

1 quantity Cheese Shortcrust Pastry
 (see page 95)
25 g (1 oz) butter
1 garlic clove, crushed
2 onions, sliced
500 g (1 lb) tomatoes, skinned
1 tablespoon tomato purée
1 teaspoon dried mixed herbs
1 teaspoon sugar
50 g (2 oz) smoked cheese, grated
4 rashers of streaky bacon, rinded and
 cut in half lengthways
13 black olives, pitted and halved
pepper

Roll out the pastry and use to line a
23 cm (9 inch) flan tin. Fill with foil
or greaseproof paper and baking
beans. Bake 'blind' in a preheated
oven, 200°C (400°F), Gas Mark 6,
for 15 minutes. Remove the quiche
and reduce the oven temperature to
190°C (375°F), Gas Mark 5.

Melt the butter and fry the garlic
and onions for 8–10 minutes. Chop
half of the tomatoes and add to the
pan. Stir in the tomato purée, herbs,
sugar and pepper, and simmer for
5 minutes. Set aside to cool slightly.

Spoon into the pastry case. Slice
the remaining tomatoes and arrange
on top. Sprinkle with cheese and
arrange the bacon and olive halves
on top. Bake in the oven for 30–35
minutes until the cheese is golden.

Serves 4–6

Ham and Mixed Vegetable Quiche

1 quantity Cheese Shortcrust Pastry
 (see page 95)
25 g (1 oz) butter
1 small red pepper, cored, deseeded
 and sliced
1 small green pepper, cored,
 deseeded and sliced
50 g (2 oz) mushrooms, thinly sliced
1 small courgette, very thinly sliced
75 g (3 oz) cooked ham, chopped
2 eggs, lightly beaten
150 ml (¼ pint) double cream
1 tablespoon freshly grated Parmesan
 cheese
salt and pepper

Roll out the pastry on a lightly
floured board and use to line a
20 cm (8 inch) flan tin. Fill with foil
or greaseproof paper and baking
beans and then bake 'blind' in a
preheated oven, 200°C (400°F), Gas
Mark 6, for 15 minutes. Remove the
quiche and then reduce the oven
temperature to 190°C (375°F), Gas
Mark 5.

Melt the butter and gently fry the
peppers, mushrooms and courgette
for 5 minutes. Sprinkle the ham
over the base of the pastry case, and
then top with the pepper mixture.

Beat together the eggs, cream,
Parmesan and seasoning to taste.
Pour into the pastry case. Bake in
the preheated oven for 30–35
minutes until set. Serve hot or cold.

Serves 4

Turkey and Cranberry Lattice Tart

1 quantity Shortcrust Pastry
  (see page 94)
75 g (3 oz) sage and onion dry
  stuffing mix
250 ml (8 fl oz) boiling water
175 g (6 oz) cold cooked turkey, diced
75 g (3 oz) fresh or frozen cranberries
2 tablespoons cranberry jelly
2 tablespoons orange juice
salt and pepper

Roll out three-quarters of the pastry on a lightly floured board and use to line an 18 cm (7 inch) flan tin.

Make up the stuffing mix with the boiling water, according to the packet instructions. Spoon the stuffing into the pastry case and level the surface.

Mix the turkey and cranberries with the cranberry jelly, orange juice, and salt and pepper. Spread over the stuffing mixture and press down evenly.

Roll out the remaining pastry, cut into thin strips and then arrange in a lattice over the tart. Bake in a preheated oven, 190°C (375°F), Gas Mark 5, for 30–40 minutes or until the pastry is cooked and golden brown. Serve hot or cold.

Serves 4

left: ham and mixed vegetable quiche
below: bacon, tomato and cheese flan

Spiced Lamb Tart with Apricots

10 sheets filo pastry
5 tablespoons olive oil
1 onion, finely chopped
250 g (8 oz) lean minced lamb
1 teaspoon ground cumin
1 teaspoon ground coriander
2 teaspoons chopped fresh root
  ginger
125 g (4 oz) easy-to-eat dried
  apricots, chopped
1 egg, beaten
75 ml (3 fl oz) Greek yogurt
salt and pepper

Brush each sheet of filo pastry with olive oil and then arrange in layers, overlapping at different angles, in a 20 cm (8 inch) flan tin. Scrunch up the pastry around the edges.

Heat 1 tablespoon of the oil in a large pan and fry the onion until soft. Stir in the lamb and fry until lightly coloured. Stir in the cumin, coriander, ginger and apricots. Cover and simmer gently for 10 minutes. Remove from the heat.

Beat together the egg and yogurt, season with salt and pepper and then stir into the meat mixture. Spoon into the pastry case, and bake in a preheated oven, 190°C (375°F), Gas Mark 5, for 20–25 minutes until the filling is set.

Serves 4

Bacon and Sweetcorn Quiche

1 quantity Shortcrust Pastry
  (see page 94)
15 g (½ oz) butter
6 rashers of streaky bacon, rinded and
  chopped
1 small onion, finely chopped
200 g (7 oz) can sweetcorn, drained
2 eggs, lightly beaten
200 ml (7 fl oz) milk
1 teaspoon dried thyme
salt and pepper

Roll out the pastry and use to line a 23 cm (9 inch) loose-bottom flan tin. Fill with foil or greaseproof paper and baking beans and bake 'blind' in a preheated oven, 200°C (400°F), Gas Mark 6, for 15 minutes. Remove the quiche and reduce the oven temperature to 190°C (375°F), Gas Mark 5.

Melt the butter and fry the bacon and onion until the onion is soft. Transfer to the pastry case and cover with sweetcorn. Beat together the eggs and milk, add the thyme and seasoning. Pour into the pastry case.

Bake in the oven for 30–35 minutes until golden brown and set.

Serves 4–6

right: bacon and sweetcorn quiche, chicken liver and sage tartlets

Chicken Liver and Sage Tartlets

8 slices white or wholemeal bread
75 g (3 oz) butter
1 shallot, finely sliced
250 g (8 oz) chicken livers, chopped
125 g (4 oz) open mushrooms, sliced
1 garlic clove, crushed
1 tablespoon chopped sage
3 tablespoons dry sherry or red wine
125 ml (4 fl oz) crème fraîche or
  single cream
salt and pepper
sage leaves, to garnish

Cut the crusts from the bread and trim to 8 cm (3½ inch) squares. Press into 8 deep patty tins. Melt 50 g (2 oz) butter and brush over the bread. Bake in a preheated oven, 200°C (400°F), Gas Mark 6, for 10–12 minutes until golden brown.

Meanwhile, melt the remaining butter and fry the shallot for 1–2 minutes. Add the chicken livers and fry until lightly coloured, then stir in the mushrooms and garlic. Cook, stirring, for 2 minutes and then add the sage and sherry or wine.

Simmer for 1 minute, stir in the crème fraîche or cream and cook for 2 minutes to reduce slightly. Season with salt and pepper and spoon into the bread cases. Serve the tartlets hot, garnished with sage leaves.

Serves 4–8

Sausage Pizza Slice

250 g (8 oz) self-raising flour
50 g (2 oz) butter or block margarine
7 tablespoons milk
salt
For the filling:
1 tablespoon olive oil
1 onion, thinly sliced
1 tablespoon plain flour
250 g (8 oz) can chopped tomatoes
2 tablespoons tomato purée
1 garlic clove, crushed
1 teaspoon dried oregano
125 ml (4 fl oz) milk
4 cooked pork sausages, sliced
125 g (4 oz) mozzarella cheese, diced
4 stuffed green olives, sliced
pepper

Sift the flour and salt into a bowl and rub in the butter. Stir in the milk and mix to a soft dough.

Roll out the pastry and use to line a 22 x 30.5 cm (8½ x 12 inch) shallow tin. Crimp the pastry edges.

Heat the oil and fry the onion for 2–3 minutes to soften. Stir in the flour and cook for 2 minutes. Add the tomatoes, tomato purée, garlic, oregano and milk. Season and simmer until thickened. Spread over the pastry and scatter the sausages, cheese and olives over the top.

Bake at 200°C (400°F), Gas Mark 6, for 30–35 minutes until golden. Serve cut into fingers or squares.

Serves 4

Mediterranean Quiche

175 g (6 oz) plain flour
40 g (1½ oz) margarine
40 g (1½ oz) lard
1½ tablespoons water
salt
Filling:
200 g (7 oz) can tuna in oil
1 onion, chopped
1 garlic clove, crushed (optional)
2 eggs, beaten
125 g (4 oz) medium-fat curd cheese
150 ml (¼ pint) single cream
1 tablespoon snipped chives
1 tablespoon grated Parmesan cheese
8 black olives, halved and pitted
salt and pepper

Sift the flour and a pinch of salt into a mixing bowl. Rub in the fat with the fingertips until the mixture resembles fine breadcrumbs. Add the water and mix to a firm dough. Knead lightly and then chill in the refrigerator for 15 minutes.

Roll out the pastry and use to line a 20 cm (8 inch) flan dish. Prick the base with a fork.

To make the filling, drain and flake the tuna, reserving 1 tablespoon oil. Heat this oil in a pan, add the onion and garlic and fry until soft.

Place in the pastry case with the flaked tuna.

Blend the eggs, curd cheese and cream, and stir in the chives and salt and pepper to taste. Pour into the flan case, sprinkle with the Parmesan and then arrange the olive halves on top.

Bake in a preheated oven, 190°C (375°F), Gas Mark 5, for 40–45 minutes or until firm and golden. Serve the quiche hot or cold.

Serves 4

below: Mediterranean quiche
right: *seafood flan*

Seafood Flan

For a cheaper dish, replace the shellfish with white fish and canned shrimps.

425 g (14 oz) Shortcrust Pastry
  (see page 94)
50 g (2 oz) butter
1 bunch of spring onions, trimmed
  and sliced
175 g (6 oz) can crabmeat
250 g (8 oz) cooked peeled prawns
2 tablespoons dry white wine
3 eggs
1 egg yolk
150 ml (¼ pint) single cream
1 tablespoon tomato purée
salt and pepper
25 g (1 oz) Gruyère cheese, grated

Roll out the pastry and use to line a 20 cm (8 inch) flan dish. Fill with foil or greaseproof paper and baking beans and then bake 'blind' in a preheated oven, 180°C (350°F), Gas Mark 4, for 15–20 minutes. Remove the foil or paper and beans.

Meanwhile, melt the butter in a pan and add the spring onions. Cook gently for 5–7 minutes but do not allow the onions to brown. Add the crabmeat and prawns and cook for a further 2 minutes, stirring gently. Add the wine and allow the mixture to boil for 2–3 minutes, then set aside to cool.

Beat together the eggs, egg yolk, cream and tomato purée. Stir in the shellfish mixture with a little salt and pepper. Pour the mixture into the pastry case, sprinkle over the cheese and bake in a preheated oven, 160°C (325°F), Gas Mark 3, for 30–35 minutes or until the filling is set and golden brown. Serve with buttered leaf spinach.

Serves 6

Creamy Kipper Brunch Flan

1 quantity Shortcrust Pastry
  (see page 94)
125 g (4 oz) long-grain rice
375 g (12 oz) cooked kipper fillets,
  sliced
2 hard-boiled eggs
125 ml (4 fl oz) single cream
1 teaspoon mild curry paste
1 tablespoon chopped parsley
salt and pepper
To garnish:
chopped fresh parsley
lemon slices

Roll out the pastry on a lightly floured board and then use to line a 23 cm (9 inch) fluted flan tin. Fill with foil or greaseproof paper and baking beans and bake 'blind' in a preheated oven, 200°C (400°F), Gas Mark 6, for 15 minutes. Remove the foil or paper and beans and bake for a further 15 minutes or until crisp and golden.

Cook the rice in boiling lightly salted water for 12–15 minutes or until tender. Drain well and mix with the kippers.

Chop the eggs and stir into the rice mixture with the cream, curry paste, parsley, and salt and pepper. Spoon into the pastry case and spread evenly. Garnish with parsley and lemon slices and serve hot.

Serves 4–6

Curried Prawn Tartlets

50 g (2 oz) butter

50 g (2 oz) plain flour

2 teaspoons curry paste or curry powder

600 ml (1 pint) milk

few drops of anchovy essence

400 g (13 oz) shortcrust pastry, thawed if frozen

375 g (12 oz) cooked peeled prawns

salt and pepper

To garnish:

20 cooked peeled prawns

paprika

20 small sprigs of parsley

Melt the butter in a pan, then stir in the flour and curry paste or powder. Cook over a low heat for 2–3 minutes. Remove the pan from the heat and gradually incorporate the milk. Return the sauce to the heat and bring gently to simmering point, stirring all the time. Simmer gently for 4–5 minutes.

Add a little anchovy essence, then pour the sauce into a mixing bowl and cover with clingfilm while cooling to prevent a skin forming.

Meanwhile, roll out the pastry and cut out 20 circles, using a 7.5 cm (3 inch) fluted pastry cutter. Place the circles in tartlet tins, prick the bases and fill with greaseproof paper or foil and baking beans. Bake 'blind' in a preheated oven, 190°C (375°F), Gas Mark 5, for 15–20 minutes until crisp and light golden in colour. Cool on a wire rack.

When the sauce is cold, stir in the prawns and add a little salt and pepper. Fill the tartlets with this mixture, then garnish with the reserved prawns. Sprinkle with a little paprika and add a sprig of parsley to each one before serving.

Makes 20

Tarte Pissaladière

1 quantity Shortcrust Pastry (see page 94)

1 tablespoon vegetable oil

1 large onion, chopped

1 garlic clove, crushed

425 g (14 oz) can chopped tomatoes

1 bay leaf, crushed

¼ teaspoon dried thyme

¼ teaspoon dried oregano

2 eggs, lightly beaten

125 g (4 oz) Gruyère or Emmenthal cheese, grated

50 g (2 oz) can anchovies, drained

6 black olives, pitted

salt and pepper

Roll out the pastry on a lightly floured board and then use to line a 22 cm (8½ inch) flan tin. Fill with foil or greaseproof paper and baking beans and then bake 'blind' in a preheated oven, 200°C (400°F), Gas Mark 6, for 15 minutes. Remove the pastry case and reduce the oven temperature to 190°C (375°F), Gas Mark 5.

Heat the oil and gently fry the onion until soft. Add the garlic, tomatoes, herbs and salt and pepper to taste. Cook over a low heat for

20–30 minutes, stirring occasionally. Remove from the heat and then stir in the beaten eggs and cheese.

Pour into the pastry case and carefully arrange the anchovies and olives on top. Bake in the preheated oven for 25–30 minutes until set and golden brown. Serve hot.

Serves 4

Mussel Tartlets

200 g (7 oz) puff pastry, thawed if
   frozen
1.5 litres (2½ pints) mussels
75 g (3 oz) butter
2 shallots, chopped
1 garlic clove, crushed
200 ml (7 fl oz) water
7 tablespoons dry white wine
2 tablespoons finely chopped parsley
25 g (1 oz) flour
2 egg yolks
200 ml (7 fl oz) double cream
salt and pepper
chopped fresh parsley, to garnish

Roll out the pastry on a lightly floured board and then use to line 6–8 tartlet tins. Fill with foil or some greaseproof paper and baking beans and then bake 'blind' in a preheated oven, 220°C (425°F), Gas Mark 7, for 10–12 minutes. Remove the baking beans and foil or paper and return the tartlet cases to the oven for a further 3 minutes.

Wash the mussels in cold water, scraping off any barnacles and removing the beards. Immerse in a bowl of cold water and discard any that open up or are cracked. Drain.

Melt half of the butter in a large, deep saucepan and briskly fry the shallots and garlic for 1 minute. Add the mussels, water, wine and parsley, and season to taste. Cover the pan and boil until the mussels open. Drain the mussels, discarding any that have not opened. Strain and reserve the cooking liquid.

Melt the remaining butter and stir in the flour. Cook, stirring constantly, for 1 minute. Gradually stir in 300 ml (½ pint) of the reserved cooking liquid. Simmer, stirring all the time, until thick and smooth. Stir in the egg yolks and cream but do not allow to boil.

Remove the pan from the heat and season to taste with salt and pepper.

Remove the mussels from their shells and divide equally between the tartlet cases. Pour the sauce over them and heat through under a preheated moderate grill. Garnish with parsley and serve hot.

Serves 6–8

*left: curried prawn tartlets
above: tarte pissaladière*

Creamy Scallop and Emmental Tart

1 quantity Rich Shortcrust Pastry
  (see page 94)
2 shallots, finely chopped
25 g (1 oz) butter
8 large scallops, with corals
1 tablespoon chopped parsley
75 g (3 oz) Emmental cheese, grated
2 eggs, beaten
150 ml (¼ pint) single cream
1 tablespoon chopped coriander
salt and pepper

Roll out the pastry and use to line a 23 cm (9 inch) fluted flan tin. Fill with foil or greaseproof paper and baking beans and bake 'blind' in a preheated oven, 200°C (400°F), Gas Mark 6, for 15 minutes. Remove and reduce the oven temperature to 180°C (350°F), Gas Mark 4.

Fry the shallots in the butter until softened. Remove the orange corals from the scallops and slice the white flesh. Stir the white flesh and corals into the shallots with the parsley, coriander, and seasoning.

Spoon the scallop mixture into the pastry case and sprinkle with cheese. Beat together the eggs and cream and pour into the pastry case. Bake in the preheated oven for 25–30 minutes or until set.

Serves 4–6

Smoked Salmon and Minted Cucumber Cream Flans

1 quantity Shortcrust Pastry
  (see page 94)
175 g (6 oz) cucumber, peeled and
  finely chopped
125 g (4 oz) cream cheese
4 tablespoons mayonnaise
2 tablespoons chopped mint
75 g (3 oz) smoked salmon
  trimmings, chopped
salt and pepper
To garnish:
cucumber slices
sprigs of mint

Roll out the pastry and use to line 12 deep patty tins or small fluted flan tins. Prick the bases with a fork and bake in a preheated oven, 200°C (400°F), Gas Mark 6, for 15 minutes. Allow to cool.

Place the cucumber in a colander and leave to drain for 30 minutes.

Beat together the cream cheese and mayonnaise until smooth, and then stir in the mint, drained cucumber and smoked salmon. Season to taste with salt and pepper.

Spoon the filling into the cooled pastry cases and then smooth over to level the tops. Garnish with cucumber and mint and serve cold.

Serves 4–6

Smoked Salmon Quiche

1 quantity Cheese Shortcrust Pastry
  (see page 95)
250 g (8 oz) cream cheese, softened
4 eggs, lightly beaten
4 egg yolks, lightly beaten
2 tablespoons lemon juice
175 g (6 oz) smoked salmon, cut into
  thin strips
300 ml (½ pint) single cream
½ teaspoon cayenne pepper
pepper
sprigs of dill, to garnish

Roll out the pastry on a lightly floured board and use to line a 28 cm (11 inch) flan tin. Chill in the refrigerator for 15 minutes.

Put the cream cheese in a bowl and gradually beat in the eggs and egg yolks. Stir in the lemon juice, smoked salmon and cream. Add the cayenne and some pepper. Pour into the pastry case.

Bake the quiche in a preheated oven, 190°C (375°F), Gas Mark 5, for 30–35 minutes until the pastry is cooked and crisp and the filling is set and golden brown and set. Serve hot or cold.

Serves 6–8

right: creamy scallop and Emmental tart, smoked salmon and minted cucumber cream flans

Tuna, Sweetcorn and Iceberg Quiche

1 quantity Wholemeal Shortcrust
  Pastry (see page 95)

¼ iceberg lettuce, shredded

200 g (7 oz) can tuna in oil, drained
  and flaked

200 g (7 oz) can sweetcorn, drained

2 tablespoons snipped chives

2 eggs, beaten

150 ml (¼ pint) single cream

salt and pepper

Roll out the pastry on a lightly
floured surface and then use to line
a 20 cm (8 inch) square fluted flan
tin. Fill with foil or greaseproof
paper and baking beans and bake
'blind' in a preheated oven, 200°C
(400°F), Gas Mark 6, for 15 minutes.
Remove from the oven and lower
the oven temperature to 190°C
(375°F), Gas Mark 5.

Arrange the lettuce, tuna and
sweetcorn in the pastry case and
then sprinkle with the chives. Beat
together the eggs and cream, season
well with salt and pepper and pour
into the flan case.

Bake the quiche in the preheated
oven for 20–25 minutes until the
filling is set and lightly browned.
Serve hot or cold.

Serves 4

Sardine Cartwheel Flan

6 thin slices granary bread, crusts
  removed

40 g (1½ oz) butter, melted

1 egg, beaten

75 g (3 oz) fromage frais

2 tomatoes, sliced

125 g (4 oz) can sardines in oil,
  drained and halved lengthways

salt and pepper

Cut all the bread slices in half
diagonally to make triangles. Brush
a 20 cm (8 inch) flan dish with
some of the melted butter, and line
with the overlapping bread slices,
pressing down firmly. Brush with
the remaining butter.

Fill with greaseproof paper and
baking beans and bake 'blind' in a
preheated oven, 200°C (400°F), Gas
Mark 6, for 10 minutes, and then
remove the beans and paper and
bake for a further 10 minutes.

Beat together the egg, fromage
frais and salt and pepper, and spoon
into the bread case. Arrange the
tomato slices and sardines on top in
a wheel shape. Bake in the oven for
15–20 minutes or until golden
brown. Serve hot.

Serves 4

Smoked Haddock and Tomato Flan

1 quantity Wholemeal Shortcrust
   Pastry (see page 95)
250 g (8 oz) smoked haddock or cod
200 ml (7 fl oz) milk
1 bay leaf
250 g (8 oz) cherry tomatoes, halved
25 g (1 oz) butter
25 g (1 oz) plain flour
2 eggs, beaten
3 tablespoons double cream
salt and pepper
chopped parsley, to garnish

Roll out the pastry and use to line a 20 cm (8 inch) fluted flan ring on a baking sheet. Fill with some foil or greaseproof paper and baking beans and bake 'blind' in a preheated oven, 200°C (400°F), Gas Mark 6, for 15 minutes. Remove from the oven and lower the temperature to 190°C (375°F), Gas Mark 5.

Put the fish in a pan with the milk and bay leaf. Bring to the boil, cover and cook gently for 10 minutes. Drain and reserve the milk. Flake the fish and arrange in the pastry case with the tomatoes.

Melt the butter in a pan and stir in the flour. Cook gently, stirring, for 1 minute, and then gradually stir in the milk. Stir over a moderate heat until thickened and smooth. Cool slightly, then beat in the eggs, cream and salt and pepper to taste.

Pour into the pastry case and bake for 25–30 minutes. Serve hot, sprinkled with parsley.

Serves 4

left: tuna, sweetcorn and iceberg quiche
below: smoked haddock and tomato flan

Salmon Quiche

1 quantity Shortcrust Pastry
  (see page 94)
25 g (1 oz) butter
1 large onion, finely chopped
2 tablespoons chopped green pepper
200 g (7 oz) can salmon, drained and
  flaked
pinch of cayenne pepper
150 ml (¼ pint) single cream
3 eggs, lightly beaten
50 g (2 oz) Cheddar cheese, grated
50 g (2 oz) green olives, pitted and
  chopped
salt and pepper

Roll out the pastry on a lightly
floured board and then use to line a
23 cm (9 inch) flan tin. Fill with foil
or greaseproof paper and baking
beans and then bake 'blind' in a
preheated oven, 200°C (400°F), Gas
Mark 6, for 15 minutes.

Melt the butter and fry the onion
for 5 minutes. Stir in the green
pepper, salmon and cayenne
pepper, and season with salt and
pepper to taste. Cook for 2 minutes,
then allow to cool.

Mix together the cream, eggs,
cheese and olives. Stir into the
salmon and pepper mixture, and
then pour into the pastry case. Bake
in the preheated oven for about
40 minutes until golden brown and
firm. Serve hot or cold.

Serves 4–6

Avocado Seafood Tarts

150 g (5 oz) filo pastry
25 g (1 oz) butter, melted
6 crab sticks, chopped
125 g (4 oz) cooked peeled prawns
1 avocado, peeled, stoned and diced
1 tablespoon lemon juice
1 teaspoon cornflour
1 tablespoon milk
125 ml (4 fl oz) Greek yogurt
1 tablespoon chopped thyme
1 garlic clove, crushed
salt and pepper
sprigs of parsley, to garnish

Cut the filo pastry sheets into
twelve 10 cm (4 inch) squares, then
brush with melted butter and use to
line 4 individual fluted brioche tins,
in 3 overlapping layers. Bake in a
preheated oven, 200°C (400°F), Gas
Mark 6, for 5 minutes. Remove and
lower the oven temperature to
190°C (375°F), Gas Mark 5.

Mix together the crab sticks and
prawns. Toss the avocado in the
lemon juice and stir into the fish
mixture. Spoon into the pastry cases.

Blend the cornflour with the milk
and stir into the yogurt. Stir in the
thyme, garlic and salt and pepper,
and then pour onto the filling. Bake
the tarts in the preheated oven for
15–20 minutes. Serve hot, garnished
with parsley sprigs.

Serves 4

Cheesy Cod and Parsley Slice

1 quantity Shortcrust Pastry
  (see page 94) with 1 tablespoon
  finely grated lemon zest added
250 g (8 oz) cod fillet, skinned and
  diced
125 g (4 oz) mature Cheddar cheese,
  grated
2 tablespoons chopped parsley
200 ml (7 fl oz) milk
2 eggs, beaten
salt and pepper

Roll out the pastry on a lightly
floured board and use to line a
19 cm (7½ inch) square flan tin or
sandwich cake tin. Roll out the
trimmings and cut out some small
fish shapes with a cutter or knife.

Arrange the cod in the pastry
case, and sprinkle with the cheese
and parsley. Beat together the milk,
eggs, and salt and pepper, and pour
into the pastry case.

Moisten the pastry edges and
place the fish shapes around the top
edge, pressing down lightly. Brush
with some milk to glaze. Bake in a
preheated oven, 180°C (350°F), Gas
Mark 4, for 35–40 minutes or until
golden brown. Serve hot.

Serves 4

*right: salmon quiche, avocado
seafood tarts*

Savoury Pies

Chicken and Mushroom Pie

250 g (8 oz) wholemeal flour
125 g (4 oz) margarine or butter
2–3 tablespoons water
salt
beaten egg, for glazing
Filling:
1 onion, chopped
2 tablespoons oil
1 garlic clove, crushed
125 g (4 oz) mushrooms, sliced
1 tablespoon wholemeal flour
300 ml (½ pint) chicken stock
500 g (1 lb) cooked chicken, skinned
  and diced
1 tablespoon chopped parsley
salt and pepper

Sift the flour and a pinch of salt into a bowl and rub in the fat with the fingertips until the mixture resembles fine breadcrumbs. Mix in enough water to form a soft dough, then wrap in clingfilm and chill in the refrigerator for 15 minutes.

Meanwhile, fry the onion in the oil until softened. Add the garlic and mushrooms and cook gently for 2 minutes. Remove from the heat and stir in the flour. Add the stock and stir until blended. Return to the heat and bring to the boil, stirring until thickened. Add the remaining ingredients, with salt and pepper to taste. Mix well and then transfer to a 1.2 litre (2 pint) pie dish.

Roll out the pastry to a shape about 5 cm (2 inches) larger than the dish. Cut off a narrow strip all round and place on the dampened edge of the pie dish. Moisten the strip, then cover with the pastry, pressing the edges together firmly.

Trim and flute the edges, decorate with pastry leaves made from the trimmings, and make a hole in the centre. Brush with beaten egg and bake the pie in a preheated oven, 200°C (400°F), Gas Mark 6, for 30 minutes until golden. Serve hot.

Serves 4

Game Pie

This traditional East Anglian game pie is excellent served hot or cold. You can vary the game, according to what is in season and available locally.

1 large onion, finely chopped
25 g (1 oz) butter
2 partridges or 1 other small game bird or 1 pheasant, cleaned and jointed
250 g (8 oz) lean steak, cut into 2.5 cm (1 inch) pieces
2 rashers of bacon, rinded and cut into 1 cm (½ inch) strips
125 g (4 oz) mushrooms
1 sprig of thyme
1 bay leaf
600 ml (1 pint) beef or game stock
250 g (8 oz) Shortcrust Pastry (see page 94) or Easy Flaky Pastry (see page 94)
salt and pepper
1 egg, beaten, for glazing

Cook the onion gently in the butter until softened. Add the game and brown on all sides. Remove from the pan and reserve. Add the steak and brown lightly.

Spread the steak out over the bottom of a large pie dish and then arrange the game joints on top. Sprinkle with the onion, bacon, mushrooms and herbs, and season with salt and pepper. Pour in the stock, then cover with some foil and simmer in the preheated oven, 150°C (300°F), Gas Mark 2, for about 1½–2 hours until tender.

Remove the dish from the oven and allow to cool. Increase the oven temperature to 200°C (400°F), Gas Mark 6. Add a little more stock to bring the liquid to 1 cm (½ inch) from the top of the meat.

Roll out the pastry and cut out a lid to fit the dish. Cut out a strip, 2.5 cm (1 inch) wide, and lay on the rim of the dish. Moisten with water, then lay on the pastry lid, pressing it down firmly. Knock back the edges and mark with a knife in ridges. Brush with beaten egg.

Roll out the trimmings and use to make leaves or other decorations. Arrange them on top of the lid and brush with more egg. Bake in the preheated oven for 20 minutes.

Reduce the oven temperature to 150°C (300°F), Gas Mark 2, place the pie lower in the oven and bake for a further 15–20 minutes.

Serves 6

left: chicken and mushroom pie
above: game pie

43

Cornish Pasties

The traditional Cornish pasty is made with good shortcrust pastry and then filled with meat and vegetables. The meat should be raw and finely chopped by hand (not minced), and the vegetables coarsely grated so that they all cook at the same time.

¼ teaspoon salt

500 g (1 lb) plain flour

250 g (8 oz) margarine

6 tablespoons iced water

500 g (1 lb) finely chopped lean beef

250 g (8 oz) potatoes, grated

1 small piece of turnip or swede, grated

1 onion, grated

3–4 tablespoons cold water

salt and pepper

a little milk or egg, for glazing

First make the pastry by sifting the salt and flour, then rubbing in the fat with the fingertips until it resembles coarse breadcrumbs. Add enough iced water gradually to make a stiff dough, kneading lightly with your hands until it is smooth. Wrap in clingfilm and chill in the refrigerator for at least 30 minutes.

Mix the meat and vegetables together with the cold water and season well with salt and pepper.

Roll out the pastry on a floured surface to about 5 mm (¼ inch) thick and cut into 4 circles, about 20 cm (8 inches) in diameter.

Divide the meat and vegetable mixture between the 4 circles, filling only one-half of each circle. Dampen the edges with cold water, fold over the pastry to cover the filling and press with a fork or the fingers to seal the edges. (Or put the filling in the middle and then draw up the edges to the centre top.)

Brush over the pasties with milk, or a little beaten egg, and make a small slit on top. Put them on a greased baking sheet and bake in a preheated oven, 220°C (425°F), Gas Mark 7, for 15 minutes, then reduce the oven temperature to 180°C (350°F), Gas Mark 4, and bake for about 35–40 minutes. Serve the pasties hot or cold.

Serves 4

Priddy Oggies

Oggie is a West Country name for pastry. Priddy oggies, with a meat and cheese filling, were first served at The Miners Arms at Priddy in Somerset. They are both original and delicious, being first baked and then deep fried.

25 g (1 oz) butter, softened
25 g (1 oz) lard, softened
1 small egg yolk
100 g (3½ oz) Cheddar cheese, grated
2½ tablespoons water
250 g (8 oz) plain flour, sifted
600 ml (1 pint) vegetable oil
salt
Filling:
500 g (1 lb) pork fillet
1 egg, beaten
75 g (3 oz) mature Cheddar cheese, grated
2 tablespoons chopped parsley
pinch of cayenne pepper
40 g (1½ oz) smoked bacon, rinded and cut into 8 strips
salt

To make the pastry, mix the butter, lard, egg yolk, cheese and water together in a warm bowl until soft. Cool the mixture in a refrigerator until it is firm. Sift the flour and salt and rub in the cooled mixture roughly with the fingertips.

Divide the dough into 3 pieces. Take each piece and then roll it 2 or 3 times into a 1 cm (½ inch) slab, moistening the top of each slab slightly before laying them on top of each other. When finished, press down firmly on the pastry and then cut downwards into 3 pieces, repeating the rolling process twice more. Cover and then chill in the refrigerator for 30 minutes.

Trim the pork fillet and slice lengthways into 2 pieces, then beat gently with a rolling pin until flat.

Reserve half of the beaten egg, then place the cheese, parsley, salt and cayenne in the bowl with the rest of the egg and mix well.

Spread the mixture evenly over the cut sides of the pork fillet, then roll up each piece, pressing down firmly. Chill in the refrigerator for 30 minutes.

To assemble the oggies, cut each roll of pork fillet into 4 slices and wrap each one in a strip of bacon. Roll out the pastry and then cut into 8 equal squares. Lay a slice of the stuffed meat in the centre of the pastry, then moisten around the edges with a little water. Bring the pastry up and over the meat, and then press the edges together in a scalloped design. Press down the base slightly to flatten. Place them on a baking sheet and brush them with the remaining beaten egg.

Bake in the centre of a preheated oven, 200°C (400°F), Gas Mark 6, for about 15 minutes or until they are just starting to brown.

Heat the oil in a deep-fryer to 180–190°C (350–375°F) or until a cube of bread browns in 30 seconds. Deep-fry the oggies until the pastry begins to brown, then drain on kitchen paper before serving.

Makes 8

left: Cornish pasties
below: priddy oggies

Pork Pie

Meat pies of many descriptions are particularly associated with London. Pork pies are perhaps the most popular, followed by veal and ham or beef pies, but mutton and rabbit pies can also be made in the same way.

pork bones (ask the butcher for
    these)
2 pig's trotters
1 large carrot, sliced
1 onion, sliced
pinch of mixed herbs
10 whole black peppercorns
3 litres (5 pints) water
beaten egg, for glazing
Hot-water crust:
200 ml (⅓ pint) water
175 g (6 oz) lard
500 g (1 lb) plain flour
½ teaspoon salt
1 egg (optional)
Filling:
1 kg (2 lb) boned pork shoulder,
    finely chopped
250 g (8 oz) rashers of unsmoked
    bacon, rinded and chopped
½ teaspoon dried sage
½ teaspoon ground cinnamon
½ teaspoon ground nutmeg
½ teaspoon ground allspice
1 teaspoon anchovy essence
salt and pepper

First, make the stock. Put the pork bones, trotters, carrot, onion, mixed herbs, peppercorns and water in a large saucepan. Bring to the boil and skim off any foam or scum.

Simmer steadily for 2 hours, then strain, cool and skim off the fat.

To make the hot-water crust, bring the water and lard to the boil and have the flour and salt ready in a bowl nearby. When the liquid boils, tip it quickly into the flour and mix rapidly together to form a smooth dough. Add the egg, if using; it gives good colour and extra richness but is not essential.

Leave the dough, covered, in a warm place until it cools just enough to enable you to handle it easily, but do not let it get cold or it will disintegrate.

Turn the dough out on to a lightly floured surface, reserving enough to make a lid, then put the remainder into a hinged pie mould or an 18 cm (7 inch) round cake tin with a removable base. Quickly and lightly push the pastry up the sides

of the tin, leaving no cracks. If it collapses, wait a little and try again, or roll it out. Set aside.

Mix together all the ingredients for the filling and pack into the pastry case, letting it mound up over the rim a little. Roll out the lid, brush the edges with beaten egg and press it onto the pie.

Make a central hole in the top and roll out a small leaf or rose from the trimmings to cover this. Brush the pie with the beaten egg and bake in a preheated oven, 200°C (400°F), Gas Mark 6, for 30 minutes. Reduce the oven temperature to 160°C (325°F), Gas Mark 3, and then cook for a further 1½–2 hours. Cover with foil if the pie browns too quickly.

Remove the pie from the oven, cool for 30 minutes, then turn it out of the mould or tin. Brush the sides

46

with beaten egg and put back in the oven for about 10 minutes to colour the pie crust.

When the pie crust is lightly browned all over, remove from the oven, lift off the rose and, with a small funnel, pour in some of the stock which will turn to jelly when cold. Leave the pie for 24 hours in the refrigerator or a cool place before cutting and eating.

Serves 4–6

Melton Mowbray Pie

Pies of this type, which are intended to be eaten cold, were made as far back as the Middle Ages.

500 g (1 lb) pork bones
2 onions, quartered
2 sage leaves
1 bay leaf
2 sprigs of marjoram
900 ml (1½ pints) boiling water
1 kg (2 lb) leg or shoulder of pork, trimmed and then cut into 5 mm (¼ inch) dice
25 g (1 oz) butter
salt and pepper
1 egg, well beaten, for glazing
Crust:
500 g (1 lb) plain flour
125 g (4 oz) butter
125 g (4 oz) lard
150 ml (¼ pint) milk and water mixed

Place the pork bones in a large saucepan with the onions, 1 sage leaf, the bay leaf, marjoram, salt and pepper. Pour in the boiling water. Boil for 2 hours to reduce the stock to 600 ml (1 pint) of liquid, then cool and skim off all the fat. Remove and discard the bones and check the seasoning. The stock will turn to jelly as it cools.

Mix together the diced pork with 1 teaspoon salt, ½ teaspoon pepper and the remaining sage leaf, finely chopped.

To make the pie crust, sift the flour with ½ teaspoon salt, then add 50 g (2 oz) of the fat and rub in with the fingertips until the mixture resembles fine breadcrumbs.

Place the remaining fat in a pan with the milk and water and bring to the boil. Make a well in the flour and, when the liquid is boiling, gradually pour it in, stirring with a wooden spoon until it is all absorbed. Knead well and leave the pastry, covered, for 10 minutes.

Roll out the pastry to a large circle, 1–2 cm (½-¾ inch) thick. Stand a 17.5 cm (7 inch) deep cake tin, open-end up, in the centre of the pastry circle and work it up to cover the sides. Trim the top of the pie with a sharp knife. Turn the pastry-covered tin on its side and roll it a few times to smooth the outside and loosen the tin. Gently stand it up again and then work the tin out – the pastry case will remain standing.

Pack the pork mixture closely into the pastry case to within 5 mm

(¼ inch) of the top, then spoon in 2 tablespoons of the jellied stock and dot the top of the meat with the butter.

Roll out all the pastry trimmings and cut out a lid that is larger than the top of the pie case. Brush the top edges of the pie case with a little milk, press on the lid and firmly crimp the edges all round to make a raised ridge. Make a small hole in the centre of the lid and roll out any pastry trimmings to make leaves to decorate the top of the pie.

Brush the pie all over with half of the beaten egg. Bake in the centre of a preheated oven, 190°C (375°F), Gas Mark 5, for 20 minutes to set the pastry, and then reduce the temperature to 160°C (325°F), Gas Mark 3, and cover the top of the pie with foil. Bake in the lower part of the oven for a further 1¾ hours.

Remove the pie from the oven about 10 minutes before the end of the baking time and brush again with the remaining beaten egg. Return to the oven to finish baking.

Reheat the jellied stock until it is liquid. As soon as the baked pie is removed from the oven, carefully pour the stock through the hole in the top until the pie is full. Cool and then leave in the refrigerator to become quite cool and allow the stock to set.

Serves 6

left: pork pie

Rabbit and Onion Pie

This delicious traditional Welsh country recipe can also be adapted for chicken. Use six chicken breasts instead of the jointed rabbit and proceed as in the main recipe.

50 g (2 oz) butter
1 rabbit, about 750 g (1½ lb) jointed, or 6 joints
250 g (8 oz) ham or bacon, thinly sliced
3 onions, finely sliced
600 ml (1 pint) stock
1 sprig of thyme
1 bay leaf
salt and pepper
1 egg, beaten, for glazing
Flaky pastry:
250 g (8 oz) self-raising flour
½ teaspoon salt
175 g (6 oz) butter
1 teaspoon lemon juice
150 ml (¼ pint) iced or very cold water

Melt the butter in a large saucepan, add the rabbit, bacon and onions and fry for 5 minutes. Season with salt and pepper, add the stock and herbs and simmer gently for 1 hour (30 minutes for chicken). Cool.

Sift the flour and salt into a bowl. Rub in 25 g (1 oz) of the butter with the fingertips and then add the lemon juice. Add the water slowly, stirring all the time until a smooth dough is formed.

Bacon, Cheese and Apple Plait

250 g (8 oz) plain flour
50 g (2 oz) margarine
50 g (2 oz) lard
2 tablespoons water
salt
beaten egg, for glazing
shredded lettuce, to garnish
Filling:
1 onion
1 cooking apple, peeled and cored
250 g (8 oz) lean bacon, rinded
1 large slice bread, crusts removed
50 g (2 oz) Cheddar cheese, grated
2 teaspoons ground coriander
½ teaspoon curry powder
1 teaspoon mixed herbs
pinch of dry mustard
salt and pepper

To make the pastry, sift the flour and a pinch of salt into a bowl. Rub in the fats, then add the water and mix to a firm dough. Turn out onto a floured surface and knead lightly. Cover and chill for 15 minutes.

Meanwhile, make the filling. Mince the onion, apple, bacon and bread. Add the cheese, coriander, curry powder, herbs, mustard, and salt and pepper to taste. Mix well.

Roll out the pastry to a rectangle, 30 x 25 cm (12 x 10 inches), and trim the edges. Place the filling down the centre, then cut slanting strips, 1 cm (½ inch) apart, down each side of the pastry. Dampen the edges with water and plait the strips over the filling by taking them alternately from each side.

Brush the plait with beaten egg and then bake in a preheated oven, 190°C (375°F), Gas Mark 5, for 30–40 minutes or until golden brown and crisp. Serve hot or cold, garnished with lettuce.

Serves 4

Roll the dough out on a lightly floured board and then dab it with small pieces of the remaining butter, using a knife blade. Sprinkle with a pinch of flour. Fold the pastry towards you and pinch the edges so that it forms an envelope.

Roll as before, rolling away from the joined edge and towards the fold so that the air is not forced out. Dab with butter again, sprinkle with flour, fold towards you, and roll once more. Repeat until all the butter has been used and you have an oblong shape, about 1 cm (½ inch) thick. Roll out to 3 mm (⅛ inch) thick and a little larger than the pie dish to be used.

Fill the pie dish with the cold rabbit mixture and cover with the pastry, knocking back the edges and pressing down firmly. Make a vent in the centre to allow the steam to escape. Roll out the pastry trimmings and then cut out some decorative leaves for the top, if liked. Arrange them on the pastry lid.

Brush the pastry lid lightly with the beaten egg and then bake in a preheated oven, 200°C (400°F), Gas Mark 6, for 25 minutes. Lower the oven temperature to 180°C (350°F), Gas Mark 4, cover the pastry with some foil and then cook for a further 15 minutes.

Serves 6

Bacon and Egg Pie

175 g (6 oz) plain flour
½ teaspoon dried mustard
¼ teaspoon salt
75 g (3 oz) butter or margarine, cut into small pieces
40 g (1½ oz) Cheddar cheese, finely grated
1 egg yolk
3 teaspoons water

Filling:
8–10 rashers of streaky bacon, rinded, stretched and halved
6 eggs, separated

Sift the flour, mustard and salt into a mixing bowl. Rub in the fat with the fingertips until the mixture resembles fine breadcrumbs. Stir in the cheese, then add the egg yolk and water and mix to a firm dough. Knead until smooth and chill in the refrigerator for 15–20 minutes.

Roll out two-thirds of the pastry on a floured surface and use to line a 20 cm (8 inch) flan dish. Roll the remaining pastry into a lid.

Grill the bacon until beginning to crisp, then cool. Whisk the egg whites until just stiff enough to hold their shape. Place half of the bacon in the pastry case. Spoon two-thirds of the egg white on top and make 6 hollows with the back of a spoon. Drop an egg yolk into each hollow and then cover with the remaining egg white and bacon rashers.

Cover the pie with the pastry lid, seal and flute the edge and make a slit in the centre. Bake the pie in a preheated oven, 200°C (400°F), Gas Mark 6, for 25–30 minutes. Serve immediately.

Serves 6

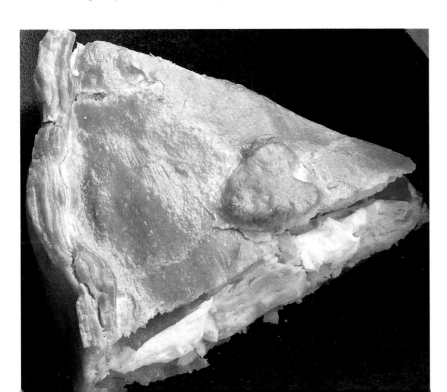

far left: bacon, cheese and apple plait
left: bacon and egg pie

Gloucester Corn Pie

250 g (8 oz) plain flour
50 g (2 oz) margarine
50 g (2 oz) lard
2 tablespoons water
salt
beaten egg, to glaze
Filling:
25 g (1 oz) butter
25 g (1 oz) flour

300 ml (½ pint) milk
75 g (3 oz) ham, chopped
½ x 325 g (11 oz) can sweetcorn,
  drained
125 g (4 oz) Double Gloucester
  cheese, grated
½ teaspoon made mustard
1 tablespoon chopped parsley
1 hard-boiled egg, sliced
salt and pepper

To make the pastry, sift the flour
and a pinch of salt into a bowl and
rub in the margarine and lard with
the fingertips until the mixture
resembles fine breadcrumbs. Mix to
a firm dough with the water, then
cover and chill in the refrigerator
for 30 minutes. Roll out two-thirds
of the pastry and use to line a 20 cm
(8 inch) pie plate.

Melt the butter in a pan, stir in
the flour and cook for 1 minute. Stir
in the milk and then heat, stirring,
until thickened. Add the other
filling ingredients, except the egg.

Place half of the mixture in the
pastry case. Slice the hard-boiled

egg and arrange on top, and cover with the remaining filling mixture.

Roll out the remaining pastry to make a lid. Dampen the edges and place the lid over the pie, sealing the edges well. Trim and flute the edges, and decorate with leaves made from the pastry trimmings. Brush the pastry with beaten egg.

Bake the pie in a preheated oven, 200°C (400°F), Gas Mark 6, for 25–30 minutes or until crisp and golden brown. Serve hot or cold.

Serves 4

Piquant Bacon Puffs

2 bacon steaks, about 250 g (8 oz)
  each, chopped
3 tablespoons mango chutney, large
  pieces of mango chopped
125 g (4 oz) Cheddar cheese, grated
1 onion, finely chopped
400 g (13 oz) puff pastry, thawed if
  frozen
beaten egg, to glaze

Put the bacon, mango chutney, cheese and onion into a bowl and stir until well mixed.

Roll out the pastry on a lightly floured surface to a 40 x 30 cm (16 x 12 inch) rectangle. Cut in half lengthways, and then cut each half into 4 squares.

Divide the filling into 8 equal portions and place in the centre of each pastry square. Dampen the pastry edges and bring together over the top of the filling. Seal the edges together firmly to enclose the filling completely and form neat oblongs.

Place the puffs, seam-side down, on a lightly greased baking sheet. Brush the tops and sides of the pie with some beaten egg and then cut 3 slashes across the top of each, using a sharp knife.

Bake the puffs in a preheated oven, 200°C (400°F), Gas Mark 6, for 30 minutes or until the pastry is golden brown, well risen and cooked through. Serve hot or cold.

Makes 8

Beef Wellington

1 kg (2 lb) fillet of beef, trimmed
40 g (1½ oz) butter, softened
1 onion, finely chopped
250 g (8 oz) mushrooms, chopped
400 g (13 oz) puff pastry, thawed if
  frozen
salt and pepper
beaten egg, to glaze
sprigs of watercress, to garnish

Pat the beef dry with kitchen paper and spread with 15 g (½ oz) of the butter. Place the beef in a roasting pan and then roast in a preheated oven, 190°C (375°F), Gas Mark 5, for 40 minutes, basting it occasionally. Remove and cool.

Melt the remaining butter in a saucepan. Add the onion and cook gently for 5 minutes until softened. Add the mushrooms and cook for about 15 minutes until some of the liquid has evaporated. Remove from the heat, season to taste with salt and pepper and leave until cold.

Increase the oven temperature to 230°C (450°F), Gas Mark 8. Roll out the pastry to a rectangle which is large enough to enclose the fillet of beef. Carefully place the pastry on a baking sheet.

Spread half of the mushroom mixture down the centre of the pastry, then place the beef on top and cover with the remaining mushroom mixture.

Brush the edges of the pastry with beaten egg and wrap the pastry around the meat, pressing the long edges together firmly and tucking in the short ends to seal. Use the trimmings to make pastry leaves to decorate the beef Wellington.

Brush all over with beaten egg, then cook in the preheated oven for about 40 minutes. Cover with foil for the last 10 minutes so that the pastry stays golden brown. Transfer to a serving dish, garnish with sprigs of watercress, and then slice and serve.

Serves 4–6

left: Gloucester corn pie

Little Mutton Pies

In 1805, a large platter of these mutton pies was served at a dinner given by the Marquis of Buckingham.

150 ml (¼ pint) red wine, boiled until reduced by one-third

300 ml (½ pint) lamb or beef stock

375 g (12 oz) lean lamb from the fillet end of a leg, finely chopped

1 onion, finely chopped

250 g (8 oz) mushrooms, finely chopped

1 teaspoon dried thyme

salt and pepper

1 egg, beaten

Pastry:

250 g (8 oz) lard (or half lard and half butter)

500 g (1 lb) plain flour

1 teaspoon salt

150 ml (¼ pint) milk and water (half and half)

Stir the reduced wine into the stock, and then add the meat, onion, mushrooms, thyme and seasoning. Simmer very gently for 40 minutes. Pour off the gravy and reserve. Leave the meat to get cold.

To make the raised pie pastry, rub 50 g (2 oz) of the fat into the flour and add the salt. Put the milk and water in a saucepan, add the rest of the fat and bring to the boil. Make a well in the flour, pour in the boiling liquid and stir thoroughly with a wooden spoon. When it is well mixed, knead the pastry and then allow to stand for 10 minutes. It should still be warm and pliable.

Divide the pastry into 8 equal-sized pieces and roll out each piece, 1–2 cm (½–¾ inch) thick. Using a 9 cm (3½ inch) individual soufflé dish, stand the dish in the middle of a pastry round and work the pastry up to cover the sides. Turn the pastry-covered dish on its side and roll it a few times to smooth the outside and loosen the dish. Gently work the dish out and the little pie shell will remain standing.

Trim the top to even it with a sharp knife. Repeat with the other pastry rounds. Roll out all the pastry trimmings and then use to cut out 8 lids, a little bigger than the diameter of the pies.

Skim off any fat from the top of the cold gravy. Fill the pies with the meat mixture and put a spoonful of gravy into each one. Put the lids on the pies, crimping the edges to make a ridge all round, and make a small hole in the centre of each. Brush with the beaten egg.

Bake the pies in a preheated oven, 190°C (375°F), Gas Mark 5, for 35 minutes or until the pastry is crisp and golden brown. Heat the reserved gravy and then pour a little through the hole in the top of each pie before serving.

Makes 8 pies

Spinach and Mushroom Plait

3 tablespoons oil

1 onion, chopped

500 g (1 lb) frozen chopped spinach, half thawed

pinch of grated nutmeg

250 g (8 oz) button mushrooms, sliced

2 garlic cloves, crushed

375 g (12 oz) Wholemeal Shortcrust
   Pastry (see page 95)

beaten egg, for glazing

1 tablespoon sesame seeds

salt and pepper

Heat 1 tablespoon oil in a pan, add the onion and fry until softened. Add the spinach, nutmeg and salt and pepper to taste and cook for 5 minutes, stirring. Turn out onto a plate to cool.

Wipe out the pan and heat the remaining oil. Add the mushrooms and garlic and fry until softened. Season to taste with salt and pepper and allow to cool.

Roll out the pastry on a lightly floured surface to 30 x 35 cm (12 x 14 inches). Mark the pastry into 3 sections lengthways. Moisten the edges with water. Make diagonal slits along the outer sections of the pastry, 2.5 cm (1 inch) apart and 7.5 cm (3 inches) long.

Spread half the spinach mixture over the centre section of the pastry, place the mushrooms on top, then cover with the remaining spinach. Fold the cut pastry strips over the spinach to give a plaited effect. Press each end firmly to seal. Lift onto a baking sheet and chill in the refrigerator for 20 minutes.

Brush with beaten egg and then sprinkle with sesame seeds. Bake in a preheated oven, 200°C (400°F), Gas Mark 6, for 30–35 minutes until golden brown. Serve with salad.

Serves 4–6

Cheese and Apple Pie

250 g (8 oz) puff pastry, thawed if
   frozen

50 g (2 oz) butter

1 large onion, finely chopped

500 g (1 lb) cooking apples, peeled,
   cored and sliced

75 g (3 oz) walnuts, chopped

250 g (8 oz) Sage Derby cheese,
   sliced

salt and pepper

beaten egg or milk, to glaze

Roll out the pastry on a lightly floured working surface until it is slightly larger than the top of a 1.2 litre (2 pint) pie dish. Cut a strip from the edge and use to line the dampened rim of the dish.

Melt the butter in a frying pan, add the onion and apple and cook gently for 5 minutes until slightly softened. Layer the onion and apple mixture with the walnuts and cheese in the pie dish, seasoning each layer with salt and pepper.

Dampen the pastry strip and then cover the pie with the pastry lid. Trim and flute the edges. If liked, use the pastry trimmings to make some leaves and apple shapes to decorate the pie.

Brush with beaten egg or milk and then bake in a preheated oven, 200°C (400°F), Gas Mark 6, for 20–25 minutes until the pastry is crisp and golden.

Serves 4

left: little mutton pies
above: *cheese and apple pie*

Serve the mushroom puffs either hot or warm with the dressing.

Serves 6

Leek and Egg Puffs

1 leek, about 200 g (7 oz) washed
  and sliced
1 tablespoon vegetable oil
1 small onion, thinly sliced
½ teaspoon coriander seeds, crushed
50 g (2 oz) mature vegetarian
  Cheddar cheese, cubed
250 g (8 oz) puff pastry, thawed if
  frozen
2 hard-boiled eggs, shelled and
  halved lengthways
salt and pepper
beaten egg, for glazing

Cook the sliced leek in a pan of boiling salted water for 6 minutes, then drain and set aside.

Heat the oil in a small pan and fry the onion until golden brown. Add the coriander seeds and seasoning and then stir in the cooked leek. Allow the mixture to cool slightly and stir in the cheese. Roll out the pastry thinly and trim to a 30 cm (12 inch) square. Cut it into four 10 cm (4 inch) squares. Cut the trimmings into leaf shapes to decorate the puffs.

Brush the edges of each pastry square with beaten egg. Divide the filling between the squares, placing

Mushroom Puffs

Do not add too many pastry-coated mushrooms to the oil at a time or the temperature will drop and the pastry will fail to puff up properly.

250 g (8 oz) wholemeal puff pastry,
  thawed if frozen
18 medium-sized button mushrooms
oil, for deep-frying
Dressing:
125 g (4 oz) Stilton cheese, finely
  crumbled or grated
150 ml (¼ pint) natural yogurt
2 tablespoons chopped coriander
  leaves or snipped chives

Roll out the puff pastry to a 30 cm (12 inch) square. Cut the square into six 10 x 15 cm (4 x 6 inch) strips. Cut each of these strips into 5 cm (2 inch) squares (36 in total).

Clean the mushrooms, removing the stalks, and then place each mushroom on a square of pastry. Dampen the edges with water and place a pastry square on top. Press the edges together to seal.

Heat the oil to 180–190°C (350–375°F), or until a cube of bread browns in 30 seconds, and deep-fry the pastry squares, a few at a time, for 2–3 minutes or until puffed and golden. Drain on kitchen paper and keep them warm while cooking the remainder.

To make the dressing, mash the Stilton with the yogurt until well blended and creamy and stir in the coriander or chives.

it just off-centre, and top with half a boiled egg. Fold the pastry over to make a triangle, then seal the edges firmly and brush with beaten egg.

Place on a baking sheet and bake in a preheated oven, 220°C (425°F), Gas Mark 7, for 15–20 minutes until puffed up and golden brown. Serve the puffs very hot.

Serves 4

Feta Parcels

150 g (5 oz) butter
1 large onion, chopped
750 g (1½ lb) frozen chopped spinach, thawed and drained
250 g (8 oz) feta cheese
2 bunches of spring onions, chopped
25 g (1 oz) chopped parsley
1 tablespoon chopped dill
2 eggs, beaten
10 sheets filo pastry
salt and pepper

Melt 25 g (1 oz) of the butter and cook the onion for 5 minutes until softened. Place the spinach in a bowl, crumble the cheese over it, and then stir in the spring onions, parsley, dill, seasoning and beaten eggs, and mix well.

Melt the remaining butter in a pan. Unwrap the filo pastry sheets. Place one on the work surface and brush with some of the butter, cover

left: mushroom puffs

with a second sheet and brush with butter. Continue until 5 sheets have been brushed with butter. Brush the top sheet. (Cover any pastry that is not being used with a cloth.)

Cut the layered pastry into three pieces widthways. Divide half of the spinach mixture between the strips, leaving a 2.5 cm (1 inch) border down the long edges. Fold in the long edges, brush with butter and fold up the short edges to make parcels, 13 x 9 cm (5 x 3½ inches). Place on a baking sheet, mark the tops and brush with melted butter.

Repeat with the remaining filo pastry sheets and spinach mixture. Bake the parcels in a preheated oven, 180°C (350°F), Gas Mark 4, for 25–30 minutes until golden.

Makes 6

Vegetable Pie with Potato Pastry

This old traditional recipe was originally designed to be eaten on fast days when meat was forbidden by the Church.

175 g (6 oz) butter or soft margarine
250 g (8 oz) self-raising flour
1 teaspoon salt
250 g (8 oz) cold cooked mashed potato
1 tablespoon milk
1 egg yolk, beaten

Filling:
250 g (8 oz) mixed vegetables, either frozen or fresh diced, cooked until just tender and allowed to cool
125 g (4 oz) mushrooms, sliced, lightly fried and allowed to cool
2 onions, finely sliced, lightly fried and allowed to cool
150 ml (¼ pint) White Sauce (see page 95)
75 g (3 oz) grated Cheddar cheese
salt and pepper

Rub the fat into the flour with the fingertips, stir in the salt and work into the mashed potato, adding the milk a little at a time.

Knead on a lightly floured board until the dough is smooth and fairly soft. Roll out the pastry and use to line a large, shallow, ovenproof dish. Fill with foil or greaseproof paper and baking beans and bake 'blind' in a preheated oven, 200°C (400°F), Gas Mark 6, for 15 minutes or until it is a light golden brown.

While the pastry is cooking, mix all the vegetables into the white sauce and season to taste.

Remove the pastry from the oven, allow to cool a little and then fill with the vegetable mixture, spreading with a palette knife so that it is smooth and flat. Sprinkle with the grated cheese.

Brush the edges of the pastry lightly with the beaten egg yolk and then return to the oven for about 15 minutes or until the cheese melts and begins to brown.

Serves 4

Stargazey Pie

This Cornish pie is probably so called because the fishes' heads are left outside the pastry, gazing upwards. Originally they were arranged like this because the oil drained back into the pie, so nothing was wasted. However, in some parts of Cornwall, a mashed potato crust is used instead of pastry.

6 tablespoons fresh white
  breadcrumbs
150 ml (¼ pint) milk
2 tablespoons chopped parsley
3 tablespoons lemon juice
grated rind of 1 lemon
1 onion, chopped
6 pilchards, herrings or mackerel, cleaned and filleted, with the heads left on
2 hard-boiled eggs, chopped
1 rasher of bacon, rinded and
  chopped
150 ml (¼ pint) dry cider
250 g (8 oz) Easy Flaky Pastry (see
  page 94)
salt and pepper

To make the stuffing, soak the breadcrumbs in the milk and leave to swell a little. Add the parsley, lemon juice and rind and onion and mix well together.

Divide the stuffing between the fish, spreading it on the flat fillets. Fold them over, then put into a round ovenproof pie dish, tails downwards and with the heads on the edge. Put the chopped eggs and bacon all around and in between the fish. Add the cider and season with salt and pepper.

Roll out the pastry to fit the dish. Press on firmly, leaving the fish heads exposed on the rim. Bake in a preheated oven, 220°C (425°F), Gas Mark 7, for 15 minutes and then reduce the oven temperature to 190°C (375°F), Gas Mark 5, and cook for a further 25 minutes.

Serves 4–6

below: stargazey pie
right: Cape Cod pie

Egg and Sardine Jalousie

400 g (13 oz) puff pastry, thawed if
　frozen
4 hard-boiled eggs, chopped
125 g (4 oz) can sardines in oil,
　drained
1–2 tablespoons curry powder
1 tablespoon chopped parsley
4 tablespoons mayonnaise
salt and pepper
beaten egg, for glazing

Roll out the pastry into a 30 cm
(12 inch) square, and then cut in
half. Place one piece of pastry on a
greased baking sheet.

Mix together the remaining
ingredients, adding salt and pepper
to taste. Spread over the pastry on
the baking sheet, leaving a 1 cm
(½ inch) border around the edge.
Brush the edges with water and
place the remaining pastry on top.
Seal and flute the edges, and brush
with beaten egg. Decorate with
shapes cut from the trimmings.

Make some cuts across the top of
the pie, about 5 mm (¼ inch) apart.

Bake the pie on the top shelf of a
preheated oven, 220°C (425°F), Gas
Mark 8, for 15 minutes. Serve hot.

Serves 4

Cape Cod Pie

500 g (1 lb) cod fillets
250 ml (8 fl oz) milk
50 g (2 oz) butter
75 g (3 oz) button mushrooms, sliced
40 g (1½ oz) plain flour
75 g (3 oz) cooked peeled prawns,
　coarsely chopped
400 g (13 oz) puff pastry, thawed if
　frozen
salt and pepper
beaten egg, to glaze

Place the cod in a saucepan, add the
milk and cook gently over a low
heat for 10 minutes until tender.
Drain, reserving the cooking liquid
in a measuring jug. Make up to
250 ml (8 fl oz) with water. Flake

the cod finely, discarding the skin
and bones.

Melt the butter, then add the
mushrooms and cook for 3 minutes.
Add the flour and cook for 1 minute.
Gradually add the reserved cooking
liquid and bring to the boil, stirring.
Simmer gently for 2–3 minutes.
Remove from the heat and stir in
the flaked fish, prawns and salt and
pepper to taste. Leave to cool.

Roll out the pastry on a lightly
floured board and then trim to a
40 x 25 cm (16 x 10 inch) rectangle,
reserving the trimmings. Cut the
pastry rectangle in half to give two
20 x 25 cm (8 x 10 inch) pieces.

Place one piece of pastry on a
dampened baking sheet. Spoon the
cold fish mixture on top and spread
out evenly to within 1.5 cm (¾ inch)
of the edges. Roll out the remaining
piece of pastry to a rectangle,
28 x 23 m (11 x 9 inch).

Dampen the edges of the pastry
on the baking sheet and cover with
the larger piece of pastry. Press the
edges firmly together to seal. Knock
up and flute the edges neatly. Make
a small hole in the centre of the pie
and brush with beaten egg.

Re-roll the pastry trimmings and
cut out some pastry leaves. Use
them to decorate the pie and brush
with more beaten egg. Cook in a
preheated oven, 200°C (400°F), Gas
Mark 6, for 30–35 minutes until
golden brown and cooked through.
Serve at once.

Serves 4

Sweet Tarts

Almond and Peach Tart

200 g (7 oz) plain flour
100 g (3½ oz) butter, softened
75 g (3 oz) sugar
1 egg yolk
2 tablespoons cold water
Filling:
75 g (3 oz) butter
40 g (1½ oz) caster sugar
2 egg yolks
65 g (2½ oz) ground almonds
1 tablespoon cornflour
425 g (14 oz) can peach halves
pinch of salt

Butter a deep 22 cm (8½ inch) flan dish or tart pan. To make the pastry, sift the flour into a bowl. Dice the butter into the flour and rub in with the fingertips until the mixture resembles fine breadcrumbs. Stir in the sugar, followed by the egg yolk. Mix to a dough with the cold water and leave to rest in the refrigerator for 30 minutes. Roll the dough out on a lightly floured surface and use it to line the prepared flan dish or pan.

To make the filling, cream the butter, add the sugar and egg yolks and beat well with a wooden spoon. Stir in the ground almonds with the cornflour and a pinch of salt.

Prick the pastry base with a fork. Spread the filling over the base of the tart and then arrange the peach halves on top, cut-side down. Press the fruit down with your fingertips.

Bake in a preheated oven, 190°C (375°F), Gas Mark 5, for 30 minutes. Serve warm or cold. If you do not intend to eat this tart immediately, do not place it in the refrigerator – the pastry will go soft. Store in an airtight tin in a cool place.

Serves 6

Pear Tart

200 g (7 oz) plain flour
100 g (3½ oz) butter, softened
3 tablespoons cold milk
salt
Filling:
250 ml (8 fl oz) double cream
2 egg yolks
2 tablespoons caster sugar
1 tablespoon Calvados or sherry
4 large pears, peeled

Butter a deep 22 cm (8½ inch) flan dish or tart pan. To make the pastry, sift the flour and a pinch of salt into a bowl. Dice the butter into the flour and rub in with the fingertips, then mix to a dough with the milk. Cover the pastry and leave to rest in the refrigerator for 20 minutes.

Roll out the pastry on a lightly floured surface and use it to line the prepared flan dish or tart pan. Prick the base lightly with a fork, fill with some foil or greaseproof paper and baking beans, and bake 'blind in a preheated oven, 200°C (400°F), Gas Mark 6, for about 10 minutes until the pastry has begun to form a slight crust.

To make the filling, beat together the cream, egg yolks, sugar and Calvados or sherry.

Halve the pears and remove the cores with a teaspoon. Make vertical slices in the pear halves without cutting all the way through. Place them, flat-side down, in the pastry case. Cover the pears with the filling mixture and return to the oven for 30 minutes.

Serves 6

Fig Tart

200 g (7 oz) plain flour
100 g (3½ oz) butter
3 tablespoons cold water
salt
Filling:
150 ml (¼ pint) milk
2 egg yolks
2 tablespoons caster sugar
1 tablespoon cornflour
250 g (8 oz) dried figs, sliced
2 tablespoons apricot jam
1 tablespoon water

Butter a 22 cm (8½ inch) flan dish or tart pan. Sift the flour and a pinch of salt into a mixing bowl. Dice the butter into the flour and rub in with the fingertips until the mixture resembles fine breadcrumbs, then mix to a dough with the cold water.

Roll out the pastry on a lightly floured surface and use to line the prepared flan dish or tart pan. Fill with foil or greaseproof paper and some baking beans and bake 'blind' in a preheated oven, 200°C (400°F), Gas Mark 6, for 15 minutes until the pastry has formed a slight crust. Remove the foil or paper and the baking beans.

To make the filling, boil the milk in a small pan. Meanwhile, whisk together the egg yolks, sugar and cornflour in a bowl. Pour the hot milk onto the mixture and stir well. Return to the pan and cook slowly until it thickens, stirring all the time with a wooden spoon. Set aside to cool.

Spread this pastry cream over the base of the pastry case. Arrange the sliced figs over the pastry cream, letting the cream show through.

Boil the apricot jam with the water in a small pan until smooth and thick, then brush this lightly over the figs and return to the oven for a further 10 minutes. Serve cold.

Serves 6

above: almond and peach tart, pear tart

Orange Tart

200 g (7 oz) plain flour
100 g (3½ oz) butter, softened
3 tablespoons cold water
Filling:
300 ml (½ pint) milk
grated rind and juice of
   3 oranges
2 whole eggs
3 egg yolks
125 g (4 oz) caster sugar
40 g (1½ oz) plain flour, sifted
To decorate:
1 orange, sliced
whipped cream

Butter a 22 cm (8½ inch) round flan dish or tart pan. To make the pastry, sift the flour into a bowl. Dice the butter into the flour and rub in with the fingertips until the mixture resembles fine breadcrumbs. Mix to a dough with the cold water.

Roll out the dough on a lightly floured surface and use it to line the prepared flan dish or tart pan. Leave to chill in the refrigerator.

To make the filling, boil the milk, then add the grated orange rind and remove from the heat. In a bowl, beat together the eggs and egg yolks with the sugar until pale. Stir in the sifted flour, a little at a time. Add the juice of the oranges. Finally, stir in the warm milk. Leave until cold.

Pour the cold orange filling into the cold unbaked pastry case. Bake in a preheated oven, 190°C (375°F), Gas Mark 5, for 40 minutes. Serve warm, decorated with slices of fresh orange and piped whipped cream.

Serves 6

Plum Tart

200 g (7 oz) plain flour
100 g (3½ oz) butter
3 tablespoons cold water
salt
1 tablespoon icing sugar
Filling:
1 kg (2 lb) yellow plums, halved, pits
   reserved
300 g (10 oz) caster sugar
4 eggs
150 g (5 oz) plain flour
150 ml (¼ pint) milk
2 tablespoons plum brandy, brandy or
   Calvados
icing sugar, sifted, to serve

Butter a 22 cm (8½ inch) flan dish or tart pan. To make the pastry, sift the flour and a pinch of salt into a bowl. Dice the butter into the flour and rub in with the fingertips until the mixture resembles fine breadcrumbs, then mix to a dough with the cold water.

Roll out the dough on a lightly floured surface and use it to line the prepared flan dish or tart pan. Prick the base lightly with a fork, fill with foil or greaseproof paper and bake 'blind' in a preheated oven, 200°C (400°F), Gas Mark 6, for 10 minutes until the pastry has begun to form a slight crust.

To make the filling, tie up the plum pits in muslin and pound the bag briefly with a rolling pin to crack the pits. Place the bag in a pan with the plums, 200 g (7 oz) caster sugar and a little water and cook gently for 15 minutes. Drain the fruit and discard the bag of pits.

Beat the eggs and add the flour, milk and the remaining sugar. Stir in the plum brandy, brandy or the Calvados.

Arrange the drained fruit in the pastry case and then pour the egg mixture over the top. Return the tart to the preheated oven for 30 minutes. Serve cool, sprinkled with icing sugar.

Serves 6

left: orange tart
right: raspberry tart

Raspberry Tart

200 g (7 oz) plain flour

100 g (3½ oz) butter

1 tablespoon caster sugar

1 egg, beaten

2 tablespoons cold water

salt

Filling:

250 g (8 oz) cream cheese

1 tablespoon sugar

500 g (1 lb) fresh raspberries

Glaze:

3 tablespoons redcurrant jelly

1 tablespoon Cointreau

Butter a 22 cm (8 inch) flan dish or tart pan. To make the pastry, sift the flour and a pinch of salt into a bowl. Dice the butter into the flour and then rub in with the fingertips until the mixture resembles fine breadcrumbs. Stir in the sugar and bind with the egg. Mix to a dough with the cold water.

Leave the dough to rest in a cool place for 20 minutes before rolling it out on a lightly floured surface. Use to line the prepared flan dish or tart pan. Prick the base lightly with a fork and then fill with foil or greaseproof paper and baking beans. Bake 'blind' in a preheated oven, 200°C (400°F), Gas Mark 6, for about 15 minutes until the pastry has begun to form a crust. Remove the foil and return the flan dish or tart pan to the oven for a further 5–10 minutes until it is completely cooked. Leave the pastry case to cool completely.

For the filling, beat together the cream cheese and sugar. Spread over the pastry case, and then cover with the raspberries.

To make the glaze, melt the redcurrant jelly in a small pan and then boil until smooth, stirring all the time. Add the Cointreau. Brush the fruit in the tart with the glaze and serve cold. Eat within 24 hours.

Serves 6

Banana and Coconut Tart

200 g (7 oz) plain flour
100 g (3½ oz) butter
3 tablespoons cold water
salt

Filling:
7 tablespoons milk
75 g (3 oz) caster sugar
100 g (3½ oz) desiccated coconut
2 eggs, beaten
1 tablespoon rum
5 bananas, sliced
4 tablespoons lemon juice

Syrup:
1 tablespoon rum
4 tablespoons sugar

To decorate:
150 ml (¼ pint) double cream, whipped
8 maraschino cherries

Butter a 22 cm (8½ inch) flan dish or tart pan. To make the pastry, sift the flour and a pinch of salt into a bowl. Dice the butter into the flour and then rub in with the fingertips until the mixture resembles fine breadcrumbs. Mix to a dough with the cold water.

Roll out the dough on a lightly floured surface and use to line the prepared flan dish or tart pan. Prick the base lightly with a fork, fill with foil or greaseproof paper and baking beans and then bake 'blind' in a preheated oven, 200°C (400°F), Gas Mark 6, for about 15 minutes until the pastry has begun to form a slight crust. Remove the foil or paper and beans from the pastry and then replace in the oven for a further 10 minutes until completely baked.

To make the filling, boil the milk in a small pan and leave to cool slightly. Mix together the sugar and the coconut, then stir in the beaten eggs. Add the milk, stirring, then return to the pan and thicken over a low heat, stirring constantly. Add the rum and then leave the mixture to cool.

Toss the banana slices in the lemon juice to prevent them discolouring, and then strain off the juice and reserve it.

In another small pan, make the syrup. Mix the rum, sugar and the strained lemon juice from the bananas. Heat the mixture over a low heat until the sugar dissolves, and then boil to form a thick syrup.

Pour the coconut mixture into the pastry case. Arrange the bananas over the top and then pour over the syrup. Decorate with swirls of cream and the cherries. Serve the tart at room temperature.

Serves 6–8

left: banana and coconut tart
right: damson tart

Damson Tart

200 g (7 oz) plain flour

100 g (3½ oz) butter

1 tablespoon sugar

1 egg, beaten

2 tablespoons cold water

Filling:

500 g (1 lb) damsons or plums,
  halved and pitted

2 tablespoons caster sugar

2 tablespoons redcurrant jelly

1 tablespoon water

To make the pastry, sift the flour into a bowl. Dice the butter into the flour and rub in with the fingertips until the mixture resembles fine breadcrumbs. Stir in the sugar, followed by the beaten egg, and mix to a dough with the cold water.

Leave to rest in the refrigerator for 20 minutes before rolling out on a lightly floured surface. Use the pastry to line a greased rectangular 35 x 10 cm (14 x 4 inch) tart pan with the dough and prick the base lightly with a fork.

For the filling, arrange the halved damsons, cut-side down, over the pastry and sprinkle with the caster sugar. Boil together the redcurrant jelly with the water until smooth, and brush over the fruit.

Bake in a preheated oven, 200°C (400°F), Gas Mark 6, for 30 minutes and serve hot or cold. This recipe can be adapted to make attractive little tartlets, if wished.

Serves 6–8

Apple and Orange Tart

200 g (7 oz) plain flour

100 g (3½ oz) butter

3 tablespoons cold water

salt

Filling:

1 kg (2 lb) red eating apples

25 g (1 oz) butter

1 tablespoon water

grated rind and juice of 1 orange

25 g (1 oz) sugar

2 tablespoons apricot jam

Butter a 22 cm (8½ inch) flan dish or tart pan. Sift the flour and a pinch of salt into a bowl. Dice the butter into the flour and then rub in with the fingertips until the mixture resembles fine breadcrumbs. Mix to a dough with the cold water.

Roll out the dough on a floured surface and line the prepared flan dish or tart pan. Prick the base lightly with a fork and fill with foil or greaseproof paper and baking beans. Bake 'blind' in a preheated oven, 200°C (400°F), Gas Mark 6, for 10 minutes until the pastry has begun to form a slight crust.

For the filling, core and slice the apples, leaving on the skin. Melt the butter in a pan over a low heat, then add the water, orange rind and juice and the sugar. Still on the heat, toss the apple slices in the mixture. When they have just begun to soften, remove them from the pan with a slotted spoon. Arrange the slices in the pastry case in overlapping concentric circles.

Boil the apricot jam in the pan with the apple and orange juice mixture until it is smooth – add a little extra water, if necessary. Pour this glaze over the fruit and bake for 20 minutes. Serve hot or cold.

Serves 6

For the filling, mix together most of the sugar, the cream, beaten eggs and liqueur, if using, and pour into the unbaked pastry case. Bake in a preheated oven, 190°C (375°F), Gas Mark 5, for 25 minutes.

Arrange the freshly prepared fruit on top and then sprinkle with the remaining sugar. Return to the oven for a further 10 minutes.

Serves 6–8

Amandine Tart

½ quantity Short Flan Pastry
  (see page 94)
125 g (4 oz) butter, softened
125 g (4 oz) caster sugar
3 eggs
125 g (4 oz) ground almonds
3 tablespoons raspberry conserve
To decorate:
50 g (2 oz) icing sugar, sifted
1 tablespoon water (approximately)
25 g (1 oz) flaked almonds

Roll out the pastry on a lightly floured surface and use to line a 23 cm (9 inch) loose-bottomed flan tin. Fill with foil or greaseproof paper and then bake 'blind' in a preheated oven, 200°C (400°F), Gas Mark 6, for 20 minutes, removing the foil or paper and baking beans after 15 minutes.

Beat the butter and sugar until light and fluffy. Add the eggs, one at a time, beating after each addition. Mix in the ground almonds.

Myrtille Tart

Myrte, which is used in this recipe, is the traditional Corsican liqueur and is made from myrtille berries on the island. Although it has the appearance of water, it is similar in potency to brandy and has a sweet, syrupy taste.

200 g (7 oz) plain flour
100 g (3½ oz) butter
3 tablespoons cold water
salt
Filling:
125 g (4 oz) sugar
150 ml (¼ pint) double cream
2 eggs, beaten
1 tablespoon Myrte (optional)
250 g (8 oz) myrtilles, blueberries or
  blackcurrants
250 g (8 oz) raspberries

Butter a 22 cm (8½ inch) flan dish or tart pan. Sift the flour and a pinch of salt into a bowl. Dice the butter into the flour and then rub in with the fingertips until the mixture resembles fine breadcrumbs. Mix to a soft dough with the water.

Roll out the dough on a floured surface and use to line the prepared flan dish or tart pan. Prick the base lightly with a fork.

Spread the raspberry conserve over the base of the flan case and cover with the almond mixture. Bake the tart in a preheated oven, 180°C (350°F), Gas Mark 4, for about 30–35 minutes.

Mix the icing sugar with enough water to make a thin pouring consistency and spread over the tart while still hot. Sprinkle with the almonds and return to the oven for 5 minutes. Serve warm or cold.

Serves 6–8

French Pear Tart

The grill must be very hot indeed or the caramelization will take too long and the custard will separate. Alternatively, omit the sugar, place in a preheated oven, 180°C (350°F), Gas Mark 4, for 5 minutes, and brush with apricot glaze.

½ **quantity Crispy Butter Pastry**
  (see page 94)
¾ **quantity Pastry Cream**
  (see Apricot Tarlets, page 84)
2 firm pears, peeled and cored
50 g (2 oz) caster sugar

Roll out the pastry on a lightly floured surface and then use to line a 23 cm (9 inch) loose-bottomed flan tin. Fill with foil or greaseproof paper and then bake 'blind' in a preheated oven, 200°C (400°F), Gas Mark 6, for 20 minutes, removing the foil or paper and baking beans after 15 minutes.

Spread the pastry cream evenly in the flan case. Cut the pears lengthways into thin slices. Place the pear slices neatly in circles on the custard, overlapping them slightly. Sprinkle the sugar evenly over the surface and place the tart under a preheated very hot grill until the sugar caramelizes.

Serves 6–8

far left: *myrtille tart*
above: *amandine tart*
left: *French pear tart*

Apple Strip

250 g (8 oz) frozen puff pastry,
  defrosted
1 egg yolk, beaten
1 kg (2 lb) apples, peeled, cored and
  thinly sliced
2 tablespoons water
1 tablespoon lemon juice
1 quantity Pastry Cream
  (see Apricot Tarlets, page 84)

Glaze:
3 tablespoons apricot jam
1 tablespoon water

Roll out the pastry into a rectangle,
12.5 cm (5 inches) wide. Sprinkle
lightly with flour and fold in half
lengthways. Cut a 1 cm (½ inch)
band from around the 3 open edges.
Open out the rectangle and then roll
out again so that it is 2 cm (1 inch)
wider and longer.

Place on a dampened baking
sheet, prick with a fork and dampen
the edges. Open the band of pastry
and press on to the rectangle to
make a border. Brush the border
with a little of the beaten egg yolk.
Bake in a preheated oven, 200°C
(400°F), Gas Mark 6, for 10 minutes.

Cook one-quarter of the apples
with the water over a gentle heat
until they have formed a smooth
purée. Meanwhile, prevent the
uncooked apple slices discolouring
by turning them in the lemon juice.

Spread the pastry cream evenly
over the pastry base. Cover this
with a layer of apple purée and then
arrange the remaining apple slices

in a fish scale pattern over the purée,
starting at the centre and working
outwards. Brush the pastry edges
with the leftover beaten egg yolk.

Reduce the oven temperature to
180°C (350°F), Gas Mark 4, and
cook for a further 10 minutes. In a
small pan, melt the apricot jam in
the water and then boil until
smooth, stirring with a wooden
spoon. Brush this glaze over the
apple slices. Serve hot or cold.

Serves 6–8

Apple Tart
with Almonds

200 g (7 oz) plain flour
65 g (2½ oz) butter
65 g (2½ oz) caster sugar
1 egg, beaten
3 tablespoons cold water
salt
4 tablespoons icing sugar, sifted, to
  decorate

Filling:
65 g (2½ oz) butter
1 tablespoon water
6 Golden Delicious apples, peeled,
  cored and sliced
75 g (3 oz) ground almonds
100 g (3½ oz) caster sugar
3 eggs, 2 separated
2 tablespoons plain flour
2 tablespoons Cointreau

Sift the flour and a pinch of salt
into a bowl. Dice the butter and
then rub in with the fingertips
until the mixture resembles fine
breadcrumbs. Using a wooden
spoon, stir in the sugar and then
the beaten egg. Mix to a dough
with the water, cover and leave in
the refrigerator to rest for
20 minutes.

Meanwhile, melt the butter for
the filling, add the water and lightly
sauté the apples for 2–3 minutes.

Mix together the ground almonds
and caster sugar. Beat in the whole
egg and 2 yolks, and then the flour
and liqueur. In a separate clean, dry
bowl, whisk the egg whites.

Roll out the pastry on a lightly floured surface and then use to line a 22 cm (8½ inch) flan dish or tart pan. Prick the base well with a fork. Arrange the apples in the unbaked pastry case. Fold the beaten egg whites into the almond mixture and pour over the apples.

Bake in a preheated oven, 200°C (400°F), Gas Mark 6, for 35 minutes. Sprinkle with sifted icing sugar.

Serves 6–8

Basque Apple Tart

200 g (7 oz) plain flour
100 g (3½ oz) butter
1 egg yolk
2 tablespoons cold water
salt
Filling:
6–8 dessert apples, peeled, cored and
    thickly sliced
4 tablespoons lemon juice
75 g (3 oz) butter
100 g (3½ oz) caster sugar
1 tablespoon ground cinnamon

Butter a 22 cm (8½ inch) flan dish or tart pan. To make the pastry, sift the flour and a pinch of salt into a bowl. Dice the butter into the flour and rub in with the fingertips until the mixture resembles fine breadcrumbs. Stir in the egg yolk with a fork, and then mix to a dough with the cold water.

Roll out the dough on a floured surface and use to line the prepared flan dish or tart pan. Prick the base lightly with a fork and fill with foil or greaseproof paper and baking beans. Bake 'blind' in a preheated oven, 200°C (400°F), Gas Mark 6, for about 20 minutes until the pastry is fully cooked.

For the filling, toss the apple slices in the lemon juice to prevent them discolouring. Melt 50 g (2 oz) butter in a pan and then lightly fry the apples with the lemon juice, 75 g (3 oz) sugar and the cinnamon. Cook gently until the apples are soft but not disintegrating.

Remove the apple slices from the pan and reserve the juice. Arrange in the pastry case in overlapping concentric circles. Sprinkle the apples with the remaining sugar and the rest of the butter, cut into dice. Heat the grill to high.

Boil up the reserved apple juice in a pan until it is thick and syrupy and then spoon this over the fruit.

Place under the preheated grill until the topping has caramelized. It may be necessary to protect the pastry edges with some crumpled foil to prevent them burning. Serve hot or cold.

Serves 6

left: apple strip
below: *Basque apple tart*

Breton Apple Tart

This round tart can also be prepared in a square dish and cut into rectangular portions. This method is most effective if the lattice work is made with very fine strips of pastry.

200 g (7 oz) plain flour
100 g (3½ oz) butter
1 tablespoon sugar
3 tablespoons cold water
salt
Filling:
1 kg (2 lb) Golden Delicious apples, peeled, cored and sliced
40 g (1½ oz) sugar
40 g (1½ oz) butter, diced
1 egg yolk, beaten

Butter a 22 cm (8½ inch) flan dish or tart pan. To make the pastry, sift the flour and a pinch of salt into a bowl. Dice the butter into the flour and rub in with the fingertips until the mixture resembles fine breadcrumbs. Stir in the sugar and mix to a dough with the cold water. Leave the dough to rest in the refrigerator for 20 minutes.

Remove the dough from the refrigerator and work it a little, using your hands. Flatten slightly, fold into 4 and repeat. Roll out on a lightly floured surface and use to line the prepared flan dish or tart pan. Reserve the leftover dough.

Fill with foil or greaseproof paper and baking beans and bake 'blind' in a preheated oven, 220°C (425°F), Gas Mark 7, for about 10 minutes.

Arrange the apples in the pastry case in overlapping concentric circles. Sprinkle with the sugar and butter. Roll out the reserved pastry dough, cut it into long thin strips and lay them across the tart to form a lattice design. Brush the strips with the beaten egg yolk. Return to the oven for 30–35 minutes. Serve the tart hot or cold.

Serves 6

Apple Cheese Cakes

Cooking fruit into a thick, well-flavoured purée called cheese was a preserving method which was often used in the days before the freezer.

250 g (8 oz) cooking apples, cored and diced
4–5 tablespoons water
thinly peeled rind of ½ lemon
2–3 cloves
1 x 2.5 cm (1 inch) piece cinnamon stick
1–2 tablespoons sugar
25 g (1 oz) butter

25 g (1 oz) cakecrumbs or fresh
  breadcrumbs
2 egg yolks or 1 whole egg, beaten
125 g (4 oz) Rich Shortcrust Pastry
  (see page 94)
caster sugar, for sprinkling

Put the apples, water, lemon rind,
cloves, cinnamon and sugar in a
pan. Cover and cook gently over a
low heat until softened. Remove the
lid and continue cooking to a thick
pulp, stirring frequently so that it
does not stick to the pan. Remove
the cinnamon stick.

Sieve the pulp and return to the
pan. Place over a gentle heat and
add the butter. When melted,
remove from the heat and cool
slightly, then stir in the crumbs and
egg. Leave until cold.

Roll out the pastry thinly on a
lightly floured surface and use to
line 12–15 tartlet tins. Prick the
bases and then three-quarters fill
with the apple mixture. Bake in a
preheated oven, 200°C (400°F), Gas
Mark 6, for 15 minutes or until the
pastry is crisp and the filling set.

Remove from the tins and cool
on a wire rack. When cold, sprinkle
generously with caster sugar.

Makes 12–15

Apple Tart with Redcurrants

200 g (7 oz) plain flour
100 g (3½ oz) butter
3 tablespoons cold water
salt
Filling:
1 kg (2 lb) red dessert apples
6 tablespoons sugar
3 tablespoons water
15 g (½ oz) butter
1 tablespoon Calvados
Glaze:
2 tablespoons redcurrant jelly
1 tablespoon water

Butter a 22 cm (8½ inch) flan dish or
tart pan. To make the pastry, sift the
flour and a pinch of salt into a
bowl. Dice the butter into the flour
and then rub in with the fingertips
until the mixture resembles fine
breadcrumbs, then mix to a dough
with the cold water.

Roll out the dough on a floured
surface and then use it to line the
prepared flan dish or tart pan. Prick
the base lightly with a fork.

For the filling, peel, core and slice
all but 2 of the apples. Cook the
slices with 4 tablespoons sugar, the
water and butter until they have
made a thick, smooth purée. Pour
this into the pastry case.

Core and slice the remaining
apples and then toss them in the
Calvados. Arrange them in a
circular pattern over the purée and
sprinkle with the remaining sugar.
Bake the tart in a preheated oven,
200°C (400°F), Gas Mark 6, for
about 30 minutes.

Meanwhile, boil the redcurrant
jelly and water in a small pouring
saucepan. Stir with a wooden spoon
until smooth. Remove the cooked
tart from the oven and slowly swirl
the hot red glaze over it in a spiral
pattern.

Serves 6

left: Breton apple tart
right: apple tart with redcurrants

Apple Amber

75 g (3 oz) butter or margarine, diced
175 g (6 oz) plain flour, sifted
1–2 tablespoons iced water
Filling:
25 g (1 oz) butter
500 g (1 lb) cooking apples, peeled, cored and sliced
175 g (6 oz) caster sugar
1 teaspoon ground cinnamon
2 eggs, separated

Rub the butter or margarine into the flour with the fingertips until the mixture resembles fine breadcrumbs. Add enough water to mix to a firm dough.

Knead lightly on a floured surface and roll out thinly. Use to line a 20 cm (8 inch) fluted flan ring. Line with foil or greaseproof paper and baking beans and then bake in a preheated oven, 200°C (400°F), Gas Mark 6, for 15 minutes. Remove the foil or paper and beans and return to the oven for 5 minutes. Remove and cool on a wire rack.

Melt the butter in a pan and add the apples. Cover the pan and cook over low heat until pulped. Beat in 75 g (3 oz) sugar, the cinnamon and egg yolks.

Pour into the flan case and bake in a preheated oven, 180°C (350°F), Gas Mark 4, for 15 minutes, then lower the oven temperature to 140°C (275°F), Gas Mark 1.

Whisk the egg whites stiffly, then whisk in half of the remaining sugar. Fold in the rest and pile the meringue over the apple. Return to the oven for 1 hour or until the meringue is crisp. Serve warm or cold with single cream.

Serves 6

Orchard Tart

To slice the apples evenly without cutting right through them, place the halves, cut-side down, on a work surface in front of a thin chopping board. Use a large knife, holding it horizontally, so that the board halts the descending blade.

125 g (4 oz) plain flour
50 g (2 oz) butter, softened
50 g (2 oz) ground hazelnuts
25 g (1 oz) soft brown sugar
1 egg, beaten
Filling:
4 large pears, peeled, cored and chopped
2 cm (¾ inch) piece fresh root ginger, peeled and chopped
2 tablespoons clear honey
125 g (4 oz) demerara sugar
3 tablespoons water
4 dessert apples, peeled, cored and halved

Put the flour in a mixing bowl and add the diced butter. Rub in with the fingertips until the mixture resembles very fine breadcrumbs. Add the hazelnuts and sugar, and bind with the beaten egg.

Roll out the pastry to line a 20 cm (8 inch) loose-bottomed flan tin.

Place the pears in a pan with the ginger, honey, sugar and water and then cook over a moderate heat for 5 minutes. Remove the pears with a slotted spoon, drain well and place in the flan case, crushing them slightly.

Slice the apple halves almost through, but keeping them in shape, and arrange, rounded-side up, over the flan. Reduce the pan juices until thick enough to coat and then spoon over the apples.

Bake in a preheated oven, 200°C (400°F), Gas Mark 6, for 30 minutes, then serve warm with cream.

Serves 6

French Apple Flan

175 g (6 oz) plain flour
75 g (3 oz) butter, softened
75 g (3 oz) caster sugar
3 egg yolks
few drops of vanilla essence
Filling:
1.5 kg (3 lb) cooking apples, peeled, cored and thinly sliced
50 g (2 oz) caster sugar
Glaze:
4 tablespoons apricot jam
2 tablespoons lemon juice

Sift the flour onto a marble slab or cool work surface. Make a well in the centre and in it place the butter, sugar, egg yolks and vanilla essence. Using the fingertips of one hand, work these ingredients together and then draw in the flour. Knead lightly until smooth and chill in the refrigerator for 1 hour.

Roll out the pastry very thinly and use to line a 25 cm (10 inch) fluted flan ring. Fill the pastry case generously with sliced apples, then arrange an overlapping layer of apples on top and sprinkle with the sugar. Bake the flan in a preheated oven, 190°C (375°F), Gas Mark 5, for 35–40 minutes.

Meanwhile, make the glaze. Heat the apricot jam with the lemon juice, and then strain and brush lightly over the apples. Serve the flan hot or cold with cream.

Serves 8

below: French apple flan

Blackcurrant Flan

175 g (6 oz) plain flour
2 teaspoons ground
  cinnamon
125 g (4 oz) butter, diced
25 g (1 oz) caster sugar
1 egg yolk
2 teaspoons water
caster sugar, for sprinkling

Filling:
500 g (1 lb) blackcurrants
125 g (4 oz) demerara sugar

Sift the flour and cinnamon into a mixing bowl. Rub in the butter with the fingertips until the mixture resembles fine breadcrumbs. Stir in the caster sugar. Add the egg yolk and water and mix to a firm dough.

Knead lightly, then roll out thinly on a lightly floured surface and use to line an 18 cm (7 inch) flan ring.

Chill the flan and pastry trimmings in the refrigerator for 15 minutes.

Put the blackcurrants and the demerara sugar in a pan. Cover the pan and cook gently over a low heat for 10 minutes, then uncover, increase the heat and cook until thick and syrupy. Turn out onto a plate to cool.

Place the fruit in the flan case. Roll out the pastry trimmings, cut into strips and use to make a lattice pattern over the fruit. Brush with water and sprinkle with caster sugar.

Bake in a preheated oven, 200°C (400°F), Gas Mark 6, for 25–30 minutes until the pastry is golden brown. Serve the flan warm or cold with whipped cream

Serves 4–6

Tarte Française

400 g (13 oz) puff pastry, thawed if
  frozen
flour, for sprinkling
1 egg yolk, mixed with 1 teaspoon
  water
Glaze:
4 tablespoons apricot jam
2 tablespoons water
1 teaspoon lemon juice
Filling:
125 g (4 oz) black grapes, deseeded
125 g (4 oz) green grapes, deseeded
125 g (4 oz) strawberries

Roll out the pastry to a rectangle, about 30 x 20 cm (12 x 8 inches).

Sprinkle the pastry lightly with flour and fold in half lengthways. Cut out a rectangle from the folded edge, leaving a 3.5 cm (1½ inch) wide band on the remaining 3 sides.

Open out the rectangle and roll until 30 x 20 cm (12 x 8 inches). Place on a dampened baking sheet, prick all over with a fork and then dampen the edges.

Open out the band of pastry and place on the rectangle to make a border. Knock up the edges and mark a pattern on the border with a knife. Brush the border with the egg yolk and water and then bake in a preheated oven, 220°C (425°F), Gas Mark 7, for 20–25 minutes.

Heat the apricot jam with the water and lemon juice, then sieve and reheat. Use to brush the base of the pastry case. Arrange the fruit in rows down the tart. Brush with the glaze and serve cold.

Serves 6

Rhubarb and Lemon Flan

The bright pink stems of forced early rhubarb are quite tender; however, later in the season the main crop tends to be a bit tougher and therefore will need peeling before use.

175 g (6 oz) plain flour, sifted
75 g (3 oz) white cooking fat or lard
2–3 tablespoons water

500 g (1 lb) rhubarb, cut into
   2.5 cm (1 inch) lengths
1 egg
175 g (6 oz) caster sugar
25 g (1 oz) cornflour
25 g (1 oz) butter
grated rind of 1 lemon
4 tablespoons lemon juice made up to
   150 ml (¼ pint) with water

Put the flour in a bowl and rub in the fat with the fingertips until the mixture resembles breadcrumbs. Add the water and then mix to a soft dough. Cover and chill in the refrigerator for 30 minutes.

Roll out the pastry and use to line a 25 cm (10 inch) flan tin. Arrange the rhubarb in circles in the uncooked pastry case.

Put the egg, sugar, cornflour, butter, lemon rind, lemon juice and water in a pan. Bring to the boil slowly, stirring all the time.

Spread the lemon mixture over the rhubarb. Bake in a preheated oven, 180°C (350°F), Gas Mark 4, for 30 minutes, then increase the oven temperature to 200°C (400°F), Gas Mark 6, and cook for a further 15 minutes. Serve warm.

Serves 4–6

Variation: This flan can be made with orange instead of lemon. Follow the recipe but reduce the amount of sugar to 125 g (4 oz) and add ½ teaspoon ground ginger, if liked.

left: tarte Française
above: *rhubarb and lemon flan*

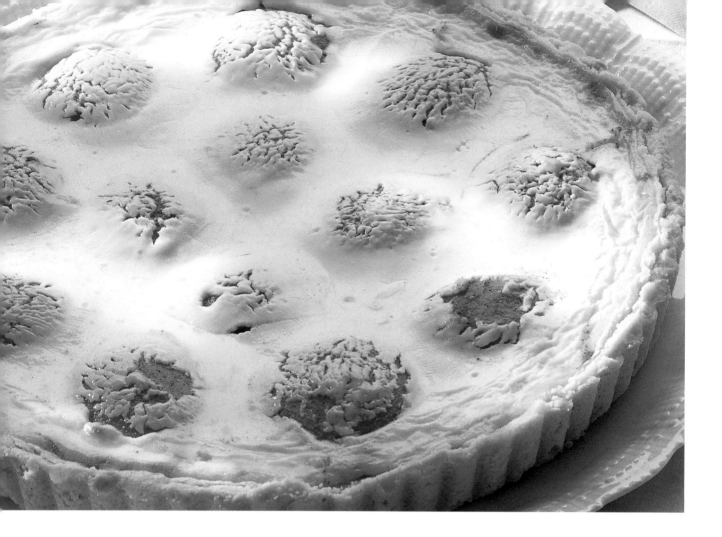

Peach Cream Küchen

250 g (8 oz) plain flour
pinch of baking powder
125 g (4 oz) butter, diced
75 g (3 oz) caster sugar
salt
Filling:
2 x 425 g (14 oz) cans peach halves,
   drained
1 teaspoon ground cinnamon
2 large egg yolks
300 ml (½ pint) soured cream

Sift the flour, baking powder and a
pinch of salt into a bowl. Rub in the
butter with the fingertips until the
mixture resembles fine breadcrumbs.

Stir in 2 tablespoons of the sugar.
Press the mixture onto the base and
sides of a greased 25 cm (10 inch)
loose-bottomed flan tin.

Arrange the peach halves in the
case. Mix together the cinnamon
and remaining sugar and sprinkle
over the fruit. Beat the egg yolks
and soured cream together and pour
over the peaches.

Bake the flan in a preheated
oven, 200°C (400°F), Gas Mark 6,
for about 30 minutes. Leave in the
tin to cool and then transfer to a
serving plate. Serve cold.

Serves 8

Linzertorte

Lattice pastry cutters will save you time
when making this torte. Roll out the
pastry and run the lattice cutter over it.

175 g (6 oz) plain flour
½ teaspoon ground cinnamon
75 g (3 oz) butter, diced
50 g (2 oz) sugar
50 g (2 oz) ground almonds
2 teaspoons finely grated lemon rind
2 large egg yolks
1 tablespoon lemon juice
375 g (12 oz) raspberry jam

Sift the flour and cinnamon into a
bowl. Rub in the butter with the
fingertips until the mixture
resembles fine breadcrumbs. Add

the sugar, ground almonds and lemon rind. Bind the pastry with the egg yolks and enough lemon juice to make a stiff dough. Turn out on to a lightly floured surface and knead lightly.

Roll out two-thirds of the pastry and then use to line an 18–20 cm (7–8 inch) fluted flan ring placed on a baking sheet. Make sure that the pastry is evenly rolled out, press to the shape of the ring and then trim off the excess pastry.

Fill the flan case with raspberry jam. Roll out the reserved pastry and trimmings and then cut it into strips with a pastry wheel or sharp knife. Use these to make a lattice over the top of the jam.

Bake in a preheated oven, 190°C (375°F), Gas Mark 5, for 25–30 minutes until golden brown. Allow to cool, then remove the flan ring and serve cut into slices.

Serves 4–6

Apple Cream Slice

½ quantity Rich Shortcrust Pastry (see page 94)
2 eggs
100 g (3½ oz) sugar
2 tablespoons plain flour, sifted
2 teaspoons finely grated lemon rind
150 ml (¼ pint) double cream
200 g (7 oz) curd cheese
1 tablespoon chunky marmalade

40 g (1½ oz) sultanas
3 green dessert apples, peeled, cored and thinly sliced
salt

Roll out the pastry on a floured surface and use to line a 20 x 30 cm (8 x 12 inch) Swiss roll tin.

Beat the eggs and sugar together until pale and thick, then fold in the flour, lemon rind, cream, curd cheese, marmalade, sultanas and a pinch of salt.

Arrange the apples in the pastry case and pour the cream mixture over them. Bake in a preheated oven, 160°C (325°F), Gas Mark 3, for 1 hour. Leave until cold and then serve cut into slices.

Serves 8–10

left: peach cream küchen
below: apple cream slice

Baked Custard Tart

250 g (8 oz) Shortcrust Pastry
 (see page 94)
4 eggs
25 g (1 oz) caster sugar
½ teaspoon vanilla essence
150 ml (¼ pint) milk
grated nutmeg

Roll out the pastry on a lightly floured surface and use to line a 20 cm (8 inch) flan case. Chill in the refrigerator for 30 minutes.

Line with foil or greaseproof paper and baking beans and bake 'blind' in a preheated oven, 200°C (400°F), Gas Mark 6, for 15 minutes. Remove the foil or paper and beans and then return the pastry case to the oven for 5 minutes.

Lightly beat the eggs with the sugar and vanilla essence in a bowl. Heat the milk in a saucepan until warm and whisk in the egg mixture. Strain into the cooked flan case and sprinkle with nutmeg.

Bake the tart in a preheated oven, 160°C (325°F), Gas Mark 3 for about 45–50 minutes until set and lightly browned. Serve warm or cold.

Serves 6

Spiced Curd Tarts

Curd cheese is a very simple cheese, made by heating milk plus an acid, such as lemon juice, very slowly until a curd forms. The whey is then drained off, usually through muslin.

1 quantity Shortcrust Pastry
 (see page 94)
50 g (2 oz) seedless raisins
50 g (2 oz) butter
50 g (2 oz) caster sugar
1 teaspoon finely grated lemon rind
1 large egg, lightly beaten
1 tablespoon self-raising flour
½ teaspoon ground cinnamon
250 g (8 oz) curd cheese
2 tablespoons milk

Roll out the pastry on a lightly floured board, then cut into 7.5 cm (3 inch) circles with a fluted cutter and use to line 14–16 patty tins. Lightly prick the pastry and then sprinkle a few raisins in the bottom of each tartlet.

In a bowl, cream the butter, sugar and lemon rind until soft and light. Gradually beat in the egg, and then the flour which has been sifted with the cinnamon. Stir in the curd

cheese and the milk. Divide the curd cheese mixture between the little pastry cases.

Bake the tarts in a preheated oven, 180°C (350°F), Gas Mark 4, for about 30 minutes or until the filling is well risen and set. Serve the tarts hot or cold.

Makes 14–16

left: baked custard tart
above: royal curd tart

Royal Curd Tart

250 g (8 oz) Shortcrust Pastry
  (see page 94)
250 g (8 oz) medium-fat curd cheese
50 g (2 oz) ground almonds
50 g (2 oz) caster sugar
2 eggs, separated
grated rind and juice of 1 lemon
50 g (2 oz) sultanas
150 ml (¼ pint) double cream
sifted icing sugar, for dusting

Roll out the pastry and use to line a 23 cm (9 inch) flan ring placed on a baking sheet. Prick the base all over with a fork.

Place the curd cheese in a bowl and blend in the ground almonds, sugar and egg yolks. Add the lemon rind and juice, sultanas and cream and mix well. Whisk the egg whites in a clean, dry bowl until stiff and then fold into the cheese mixture.

Pour into the flan case and bake in a preheated oven, 200°C (400°F), Gas Mark 6, for 20 minutes. Lower the temperature to 180°C (350°F), Gas Mark 4, and continue to cook for 30–35 minutes until firm and golden. Serve warm or chilled, dusted with icing sugar.

Serves 6

Honey and Nut Tart

200 g (7 oz) plain flour
100 g (3½ oz) butter
1 teaspoon sugar
3 tablespoons cold water
salt
Filling:
250 g (8 oz) shelled walnuts
500 g (1 lb) clear honey

To make the pastry, sift the flour and a pinch of salt into a bowl. Dice the butter into the flour and rub in with the fingertips until the mixture resembles fine breadcrumbs. Stir in the sugar and mix to a dough with the cold water.

Roll out on a lightly floured surface and line a 22 cm (8½ inch) flan dish or tart pan. Prick the pastry case lightly with a fork, fill with foil or greaseproof paper and baking beans and bake 'blind' in a preheated oven, 200°C (400°F), Gas Mark 6, for 20 minutes until almost cooked. Remove the foil or paper and baking beans.

Reserve 8 walnut halves for the decoration. For the filling, roughly chop the remainder and mix them with the honey. Pour this into the pastry case and return to the oven for 10 minutes.

Decorate the hot tart with the reserved walnut halves. Serve warm or cold with thick cream.

Serves 6–8

Flaky Honey and Walnut Layer

250 g (8 oz) puff pastry, thawed if frozen
oil, for shallow-frying
6 tablespoons clear honey
100 g (3½ oz) walnut halves, sliced
300 ml (½ pint) double cream, whipped
icing sugar, for dredging

Divide the pastry into 3 pieces and then roll out each circle thinly on a lightly floured surface into a 20 cm (8 inch) circle.

Pour oil into a large frying pan to a depth of about 5 mm (¼ inch) and heat gently until just beginning to smoke. Add a pastry circle and fry for 1–2 minutes on each side until golden and puffy. Drain on kitchen paper. Cook the remaining pastry circles in the same way and cool.

Place one pastry circle on a serving plate. Drizzle over half of the honey, scatter with half of the walnuts and cover with half of the cream. Repeat the layers and finish with a pastry round. Sprinkle thickly with icing sugar.

Heat a metal skewer over a gas flame or an electric ring until red hot. Holding it carefully with an oven glove, use the hot end to mark a pattern over the icing sugar.

Serves 4–6

Rice Tart

250 g (8 oz) plain flour
125 g (4 oz) butter
125 g (4 oz) sugar
1 egg, beaten
pinch of salt
Filling:
400 ml (14 fl oz) milk
few drops of vanilla essence
100 g (3½ oz) pudding rice
75 g (3 oz) sugar
2 tablespoons cream
1 egg, beaten
50 g (2 oz) crystallized ginger
50 g (2 oz) crystallized pineapple
2 tablespoons rum
2 egg whites, whisked
40 g (1½ oz) butter
5 sugar lumps

Butter a 25 cm (10 inch) flan dish or tart pan. To make the pastry, sift the flour and a pinch of salt into a bowl. Dice the butter into the flour and rub in with the fingertips until the mixture resembles breadcrumbs. Stir in the sugar and then the beaten egg. Mix to a dough with the cold water. Cover and chill in the refrigerator for at least 1 hour.

Roll out the pastry on a lightly floured surface and then use to line the prepared flan dish or tart pan.

To make the filling, boil the milk with the vanilla essence. Wash the rice and add it to the milk. Half-cover the pan and leave to simmer gently for 25 minutes.

Remove from the heat and stir in a pinch of salt, the sugar, cream, beaten egg, crystallized fruit and rum. Gently fold in the egg whites.

Spoon this mixture into the unbaked pastry case. Melt the butter in a small pan and pour over the top of the tart. Now crumble the sugar cubes slightly over the surface.

Bake the tart in a preheated oven, 190°C (375°F), Gas Mark 5, for about 30–35 minutes. Serve hot.

Serves 6

left: honey and nut tart
below: rice tart

Mincemeat Flan

250 g (8 oz) Rich Shortcrust Pastry
  (see page 94)
caster sugar, for sprinkling
Filling:
500 g (1 lb) mincemeat
2 dessert apples, peeled, cored and
  chopped
125 g (4 oz) grapes, halved and
  deseeded
grated rind of 1 orange
2 tablespoons brandy
To serve:
1 tablespoon brandy
150 ml (¼ pint) double cream,
  whipped

Roll out two-thirds of the pastry
thinly on a lightly floured surface
and use to line a 23 cm (9 inch)
fluted flan ring. Chill the flan and
remaining pastry in the refrigerator
for 15 minutes.

Mix all the filling ingredients
together and use to fill the flan case.
Roll out the remaining pastry thinly
and cut out about twelve 7.5 cm
(3 inch) rounds, with a fluted cutter.
Dampen the edges of the pastry in
the flan ring and arrange the rounds
overlapping around the edge.

Brush with water, sprinkle with
caster sugar and bake in a preheated
oven, 200°C (400°F), Gas Mark 6,
for 35–40 minutes until golden.

Fold the brandy into the whipped
cream. Serve the flan hot or cold,
topped with the brandy cream.

Serves 6–8

Treacle Tart

175 g (6 oz) plain flour
75 g (3 oz) butter or margarine, diced
1–2 tablespoons iced water
Filling:
250 g (8 oz) golden syrup
75 g (3 oz) fresh white breadcrumbs
grated rind of ½ lemon

Sift the flour into a bowl, then rub
in the butter or margarine with the
fingertips until the mixture
resembles fine breadcrumbs. Add
the iced water gradually and mix to
a firm dough.

Turn out onto a lightly floured
surface and knead lightly. Roll out
thinly to a 23 cm (9 inch) circle.
Use to line an 18 cm (7 inch) flan

ring placed on a baking sheet. Chill
the flan and pastry trimmings in
the refrigerator for 15 minutes.

Mix the syrup, breadcrumbs and
lemon rind together and spread
over the pastry. Roll out the pastry
trimmings, cut into long narrow
strips and use to make a lattice
pattern over the top of the filling.

Bake the tart in a preheated oven,
200°C (400°F), Gas Mark 6, for
about 30–35 minutes. Serve warm
with cream.

Serves 4–6

above: treacle tart
above right: mincemeat flan
right: pecan pie

Pecan Pie

175 g (6 oz) plain flour

125 g (4 oz) butter, diced

1 egg yolk

2–3 teaspoons cold water

Filling:

25 g (1 oz) butter

125 g (4 oz) caster sugar

175 g (6 oz) maple or golden syrup

4 eggs

1 teaspoon vanilla essence

50 g (2 oz) pecan nuts or walnuts,
   chopped

Sift the flour into a mixing bowl. Rub in the butter with the fingertips until the mixture resembles fine breadcrumbs. Add the egg yolk and water and mix to a firm dough.

Knead lightly on a floured surface until smooth. Roll out and use to line a 20 cm (8 inch) fluted flan ring or pie dish. If possible, chill in the refrigerator for 20–30 minutes.

Line with foil or greaseproof paper and baking beans and then bake 'blind' on the top shelf of a preheated oven, 200°C (400°F), Gas Mark 6, for 15–20 minutes. Remove the beans and foil or paper and then return the pie to the oven for

5 minutes. Cool and then remove the flan ring, if used.

Cream the butter and sugar until very soft and creamy. Gradually beat in the syrup, then beat in the eggs, one at a time, and vanilla essence (the mixture may look curdled). Pour into the pastry case and sprinkle the nuts on top.

Bake the pie in a preheated hot oven, 220°C (425°F), Gas Mark 7, for 10 minutes, then lower the temperature to 180°C (350°F), Gas Mark 4, and cook for 30–35 minutes. Serve cool with whipped cream, if desired.

Serves 6–8

Calvados Meringue Tart

200 g (7 oz) plain flour
100 g (3½ oz) butter
3 tablespoons cold milk
salt
Filling:
25 g (1 oz) butter
1 kg (2 lb) dessert apples, peeled,
    cored and sliced
3 tablespoons Calvados
2 eggs, separated
2 tablespoons caster sugar
1 tablespoon cornflour
150 ml (¼ pint) milk
50 g (2 oz) sifted icing sugar

Butter a 22 cm (8½ inch) flan dish or tart pan. Sift the flour and a pinch of salt into a bowl. Dice the butter into the flour and rub in with the fingertips until the mixture resembles fine breadcrumbs, and then mix to a dough with the milk.

Leave to rest in the refrigerator for 20 minutes before rolling out on a lightly floured surface. Line the prepared flan dish or tart pan. Prick the base lightly with a fork, line with foil or greaseproof paper and baking beans and bake 'blind' in a preheated oven, 200°C (400°F), Gas Mark 6, for about 10 minutes.

Melt the butter in a frying pan and sauté the apples until they are soft. Hold 1 tablespoon of the Calvados over a flame until it is hot, then light it with a match and pour it over the apples to flambé them.

Make a pastry cream by stirring together the egg yolks, caster sugar and cornflour in a very small pan. Add a little of the milk and beat until smooth. Gradually add the remaining milk and stir over a low heat until it is smooth and thick. Stir in another tablespoon of the Calvados.

Spread the pastry cream evenly over the pastry case. Arrange the apples over the top of the pastry cream, keeping the surface level.

Whisk the egg whites in a clean, dry bowl until stiff. Stir in the icing sugar and continue to whisk until the whites stand in peaks. Spread this over the apples, fluffing up the whites with a fork.

Bake the tart in the preheated oven for about 8 minutes until the meringue has begun to colour. Remove from the oven and sprinkle immediately with the remaining Calvados. Serve hot.

Serves 6–8

below: Calvados meringue tart
right: pineapple meringue pie

Lemon Meringue Pie

175 g (6 oz) Shortcrust Pastry
  (see page 94)
50 g (2 oz) cornflour
300 ml (½ pint) water
25 g (1 oz) butter
grated rind and juice of 2 small
  lemons
2 eggs, separated
175 g (6 oz) caster sugar

Roll out the pastry on a lightly floured board and then use to line a 20 cm (8 inch) fluted flan ring. Line with foil or greaseproof paper and baking beans and then bake in a preheated oven, 200°C (400°F), Gas Mark 6, for 15–20 minutes. Remove the foil or paper and baking beans and return the pastry case to the oven for 5 minutes. Remove the flan ring and cool on a wire rack.

Blend the cornflour with a little of the water in a small pan. Add the remaining water and the butter. Bring to the boil slowly, stirring constantly. Cook gently, stirring, for 3 minutes. Remove from the heat and add the lemon rind and juice, egg yolks and 50 g (2 oz) of the sugar. Pour into the flan case.

Whisk the egg whites until very stiff, then whisk in 50 g (2 oz) of the sugar. Fold in the remaining sugar and spread over the filling.

Alternatively, put the meringue in a piping bag and pipe it in swirls over the top of the filling.

Bake the pie in a preheated oven, 160°C (325°F), Gas Mark 3, for 20–25 minutes. Serve hot or cold.

Serves 4-6

Pineapple Meringue Pie

250 g (8 oz) Shortcrust Pastry
  (see page 94)
50 g (2 oz) cornflour
450 ml (¾ pint) pineapple juice
3 eggs, separated
25 g (1 oz) butter
175 g (6 oz) caster sugar
caster sugar, for sprinkling

Roll out the pastry on a floured surface and then use to line a 20 cm (8 inch) fluted flan dish or flan ring. Fill with foil or greaseproof paper and baking beans and bake 'blind' in a preheated oven, 200°C (400°F), Gas Mark 6, for 15–20 minutes.

Remove the beans and foil or paper and return the pastry case to the oven for 5 minutes. Cool and then remove the flan ring, if using.

Blend the cornflour with a little of the pineapple juice in a pan. Add the remaining juice and heat slowly, stirring, until thickened. Remove from the heat and beat in the egg yolks and butter. Pour into the pastry case and set aside to cool.

Whisk the egg whites in a clean, dry bowl until very stiff. Add the sugar, a little at a time, whisking thoroughly between each addition until the meringue is glossy and forms soft peaks.

Spoon the meringue into a large piping bag, which is fitted with a 1 cm (½ inch) star nozzle, and pipe over the pineapple filling. Sprinkle lightly with a little caster sugar.

Bake the pie in a preheated oven, 160°C (325°F), Gas Mark 3, for 15–20 minutes until golden brown. Serve warm or cold.

Serves 6

Apricot Tartlets

200 g (7 oz) plain flour
100 g (3½ oz) butter
3 tablespoons cold water
salt
Pastry cream:
2 egg yolks
2 tablespoons sugar
1 tablespoon cornflour
150 ml (¼ pint) milk
3 tablespoons apricot jam
425 g (14 oz) can apricot halves
1 tablespoon water
tiny mint leaves, to decorate

Butter 8 individual tartlet tins. Sift the flour and a pinch of salt into a bowl. Dice the butter into the flour and rub in with the fingertips until the mixture resembles fine breadcrumbs, then mix to a dough with the water.

Roll out the pastry on a floured surface and use to line the buttered individual tartlet tins. Prick the bases lightly with a fork, fill with foil or greaseproof paper and baking beans and then bake 'blind' in a preheated oven, 200°C (400°F), Gas Mark 6, for about 10 minutes until the pastry has begun to form a slight crust. Remove the pastry case from the oven and remove the foil or paper and beans.

Using a fork, mix together the egg yolks, sugar and cornflour in a small pan. Slowly whisk in a little of the milk. Place the pan over a low heat and continue to whisk while you add the rest of the milk. Stir gently until it is smooth and thick. Remove the pan from the heat.

Spread 1 tablespoon of the apricot jam over the base of each pastry case, followed by the pastry cream. Drain the apricots and arrange them in the tartlets.

Melt the remaining jam in a pan with the water and then boil until smooth. Pour or brush over the fruit. Return the tartlets to the oven for a further 5–10 minutes. Decorate with the mint leaves.

Serves 8

Lemon Tartlets

200 g (7 oz) plain flour
100 g (3½ oz) butter
1 egg yolk
2 tablespoons cold water
salt
crystallized lemon slices, to decorate
Filling:
1 egg
150 g (5 oz) sugar
grated rind and juice of 1 lemon
65 g (2½ oz) butter

To make the pastry, sift the flour and a pinch of salt into a bowl. Dice the butter into the flour and rub in with the fingertips until the mixture resembles fine breadcrumbs. Stir in the egg yolk and mix to a dough with the water.

Leave the dough to rest in the refrigerator for 20 minutes before rolling out on a lightly floured surface. Line 8–10 tartlet tins with the pastry and then prick the bases lightly with a fork.

For the filling, beat the egg with the sugar. Slowly stir in the lemon rind and juice. Soften the butter in the oven and incorporate with the lemon mixture. Pour this mixture into the tartlet cases.

Bake the tartlets in a preheated oven, 180°C (350°F), Gas Mark 4, for 25 minutes until the filling has set and the pastry is fully cooked.

Cool the lemon tartlets completely and then decorate with the crystallized lemon slices.

Serves 8–10

above left: apricot tartlets
right: fruit strip

Fruit Strip

200 g (7 oz) puff pastry, thawed if
   frozen
Pastry cream:
2 egg yolks, beaten
150 ml (¼ pint) milk
1 tablespoon cornflour
2 tablespoons sugar

few drops of vanilla essence
Fruit filling:
125 g (4 oz) maraschino cherries
1 mango, peeled, stoned and sliced
2 rings pineapple, diced
1 kiwi fruit, sliced
125 g (4 oz) raspberries
Glaze:
2 tablespoons apricot jam
1 tablespoon water

Roll out the pastry into a rectangle, about 12.5 cm (5 inches) wide. Fold it in half lengthways, then cut out a 1 cm (½ inch) band from around the 3 open edges. Open out the pastry rectangle and roll again so that it is 2 cm (1 inch) wider and longer.

Place on a dampened baking sheet, prick with a fork and dampen the edges. Open the band of pastry and press on to the rectangle to make a border. Prick the base with a fork and bake in a preheated oven, 200°C (400°F), Gas Mark 6, for 10 minutes. Reduce the oven temperature to 160°C (325°F), Gas Mark 3, and then cook for a further 15 minutes. Remove and cool.

To make the pastry cream, boil the milk in a small pan. In a bowl, mix together the cornflour, sugar and egg yolks. Pour the milk onto the egg mixture together with a few drops of vanilla essence. Return to the pan and then cook slowly over a low heat, stirring all the time with a wooden spoon until thickened. Allow to cool.

Spread the pastry cream over the cooked pastry case. Arrange the fruits in an attractive pattern over the top of the pastry cream.

To make the glaze, boil the apricot jam with the water in a small pan until it is smooth. Brush lightly over the fruits.

Serves 6–8

Sweet Pies

Galette des Rois à la Frangipane

This tart is eaten in France to celebrate Twelfth Night. It is available in all the pâtisseries and comes complete with gold and silver cardboard crowns. Inside the cake two china beans are planted; one will represent the king and the other his queen. Whichever lucky couple should find these must don their crowns and may bask in temporary glory and the privileges of sovereignty.

100 g (3½ oz) ground almonds
100 g (3½ oz) icing sugar, sifted
1 whole egg and 1 yolk
50 g (2 oz) butter, softened
2 tablespoons Cointreau
425 g (14 oz) puff pastry, thawed if frozen
2 china beans or silver coins

Make the frangipane filling by beating together in a mixing bowl the ground almonds, sugar, the whole egg, softened butter and the Cointreau.

Roll out the pastry on a lightly floured surface into the shape of a rectangle. Cut 2 circles out of this, using a 22 cm (8½ inch) flan dish or tart pan as a template. Make one circle the size of the dish, the other 2.5 cm (1 inch) larger.

Butter the same flan dish or tart pan and line it with the larger circle of pastry. Spread the frangipane over the pastry. Hide the beans or coins in the mixture. Wet the edges of the pastry with a little water and place the remaining circle on top. Seal the pastry by pressing the edges together. Beat the remaining egg yolk with a little water and brush over the surface of the galette.

Using the back of a knife, make a lattice pattern on top of the pastry and then bake in a preheated oven, 220°C (425°F), Gas Mark 7, for 20 minutes. Serve hot or cold.

Serves 6

Nutty Apple Pies

1 kg (2 lb) cooking apples, peeled,
   cored and thinly sliced
50 g (2 oz) brown sugar
¾ teaspoon ground cinnamon
¼ teaspoon grated nutmeg
125 g (4 oz) walnuts, finely chopped
375 g (12 oz) Pâte Sucrée
   (see page 95)

Mix together the apples, brown sugar, spices and half of the chopped walnuts. Divide the apple mixture between 6 individual baking dishes, about 10 cm (4 inches) in diameter and about 4 cm (1¾ inches) deep.

Divide the pastry dough into 6 portions and pat each one into a round, about 15 cm (6 inches) in diameter. Place the pastry rounds on the baking dishes and pinch over the edges to seal.

Bake the pies in a preheated oven, 180°C (350°F), Gas Mark 4, for 40–45 minutes or until golden.

Makes 6

Apple and Raisin Pie

175 g (6 oz) wholemeal flour
125 g (4 oz) plain flour
150 g (5 oz) margarine
3–4 tablespoons iced water
1 tablespoon sesame seeds
Filling:
750 g (1½ lb) dessert apples, peeled,
   cored and sliced
2 tablespoons brown sugar
1 teaspoon ground cinnamon
4 cloves
40 g (2 oz) raisins

Put the flours in a bowl and rub in the margarine until the mixture resembles breadcrumbs. Stir in the water to mix to a fairly stiff dough.

Knead lightly until smooth, then cut in half. Roll out one piece thinly and use to line a 20 cm (8 inch) pie dish. Layer the apples, sugar and spices in the pastry case and brush the pastry rim with cold water.

Roll out the remaining pastry and use to cover the pie. Seal and pinch the edges and trim off any surplus pastry. Make a hole in the centre of the pie and chill for 20 minutes.

Brush with water, sprinkle with sesame seeds and bake in a preheated oven, 200°C (400°F), Gas Mark 6, for 30–40 minutes until golden.

Serves 6

left: galette des rois à la frangipane
above: apple and raisin pie

Apple Pie with Almond Pastry

175 g (6 oz) plain flour

2 rounded tablespoons ground
  almonds

125 g (4 oz) butter, softened

25 g (1 oz) icing sugar, sifted

1 egg yolk

2 tablespoons cold water

milk, for glazing

Filling:

750 g (1½ lb) apples, peeled,
  cored and sliced

or 500 g (1 lb) apples peeled,
  cored and sliced and 250 g
  (½ lb) blackberries

2 teaspoons lemon juice

125 g (4 oz) caster sugar

First make the pastry by putting the flour and almonds into a bowl. Add the butter, cut into small pieces, and rub into the flour mixture with the fingertips until it resembles fine breadcrumbs. Add the sifted icing sugar, mixing well. Make a well in the centre and then add the egg yolk and water. Mix to a rough dough with a fork.

Turn out on to a lightly floured surface and knead gently until the dough is quite smooth. Roll into a ball and chill in the refrigerator for at least 30 minutes before using.

Divide the pastry into 2 pieces and roll out half to line a 20 cm (8 inch) shallow pie plate. Fill the pie with the apples, blackberries (if using), lemon juice and sugar. Dampen the edges and then lay the other piece of pastry on top, pressing down the edges with finger and thumb.

Make a small slit in the middle to let the air out, or prick lightly all over the top of the pie with a fork. Brush lightly with a little milk.

Bake in the centre of a preheated oven, 200°C (400°F), Gas Mark 6, for 20 minutes, then reduce the oven temperature to 160°C (325°F), Gas Mark 3, and cook for a further 15–20 minutes. Serve warm with clotted cream.

below: apple pie with almond pastry
right: spiced apple pie

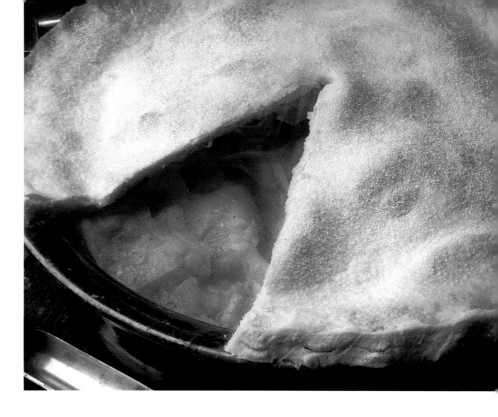

Apricot Envelope Tart

500 g (1 lb) puff pastry, thawed if
frozen
425 g (14 oz) can apricots
beaten egg, for glazing
1 teaspoon sugar
1 tablespoon icing sugar, for dusting
Almond paste:
75 g (3 oz) butter
75 g (3 oz) caster sugar
1 tablespoon plain flour
75 g (3 oz) ground almonds
few drops of almond essence
1½ eggs

Roll out the pastry into a square on
a lightly floured board.

To make the almond paste, in a
bowl, cream together the butter and
caster sugar. Add the flour and stir
in well. Add the ground almonds
and a few drops of almond essence
and then mix to a cream with the
eggs. Spread the almond paste over
the square of pastry.

Using a blender or food processor,
purée the drained apricots and
spread them over the paste. Pull up
the 4 corners of the pastry to make
an envelope. Brush the beaten egg
over each of the 4 triangles of pastry
and sprinkle with sugar.

Place on a baking sheet and bake
in a preheated oven, 220°C (425°F),
Gas Mark 7, for 10 minutes. Reduce
the heat to 200°C (400°F), Gas Mark
6, and cook the pie for a further
15–20 minutes. Just before the tart
is cooked, sprinkle it with the icing
sugar. Serve warm or cold.

Serves 4–6

Spiced Apple Pie

750 g (1½ lb) cooking apples, peeled,
cored and thinly sliced
75 g (3 oz) soft brown sugar
½ teaspoon ground cinnamon
½ teaspoon grated nutmeg
4 cloves
175 g (6 oz) Shortcrust Pastry
(see page 94)
water and caster sugar, for glazing
Crème à la vanille:
2 egg yolks
1 teaspoon cornflour
25 g (1 oz) caster sugar
300 ml (½ pint) milk
½ teaspoon vanilla essence

Layer the apples with the sugar and
spices in a 900 ml (1½ pint) pie dish,
finishing with a layer of apples. Roll
out the pastry to a circle about 5 cm
(2 inches) larger than the pie dish.
Cut off a narrow strip all round and
use to cover the dampened rim of
the pie dish; brush with water.

Lift the pastry over the apples,
sealing the edges. Trim and flute the
edges of the pastry and make a hole
in the centre. Brush the pie with
water, sprinkle with sugar and bake
in a preheated oven, 200°C (400°F),
Gas Mark 6, for 30–40 minutes.

Make the crème à la vanille. In a
bowl, cream the egg yolks with the
cornflour and sugar. Bring the milk
to the boil, pour onto the egg yolk
mixture and stir well. Return to the
pan and heat gently, stirring
constantly, until the mixture is
thick enough to coat the back of a
spoon. Add the vanilla essence and
then strain. Serve the pie hot or
cold with the crème à la vanille
handed separately.

Serves 4–6

Apple Strudel

Strudel pastry is wafer-thin, and if you have long fingernails, which could puncture the dough, you must use your fists to stretch it.

150 g (5 oz) plain flour
2 teaspoons oil
½ egg, beaten
about 125 ml (4 fl oz) warm water
25 g (1 oz) butter, melted
2 tablespoons breadcrumbs, toasted
salt
icing sugar, for dusting
Filling:
500 g (1 lb) cooking apples, peeled, cored and sliced
icing sugar, for dusting
50 g (2 oz) currants
50 g (2 oz) sultanas
1 teaspoon ground cinnamon
1 tablespoon breadcrumbs, toasted

Mix the flour with a pinch of salt in a large bowl. Make a well in the centre and add the oil, beaten egg and 2–3 tablespoons of the warm water. Start to mix, adding more warm water to make a soft paste. Beat, using your hand, until smooth. Cover and leave for 15 minutes, then knead until very smooth.

For the filling, stir together the apples with the currants, sultanas, cinnamon and breadcrumbs until thoroughly mixed.

Roll out the strudel pastry on a floured surface to 1 cm (½ inch) thick. Lift on to a floured tea towel and leave for 8 minutes. Carefully stretch the pastry until it is very thin. Brush with some of the melted butter and then sprinkle with the breadcrumbs. Scatter the fruit filling mixture over the pastry and roll up.

Place on a greased baking tray in a horseshoe shape and brush with melted butter. Bake in a preheated oven, 200°C (400°F), Gas Mark 6, for 20–25 minutes until golden brown. Dust with icing sugar and slice to serve.

Serves 6

Apple Florentine Pies

An eighteenth-century recipe from Lincolnshire and Bedfordshire, these delicious apple pies were traditionally made at Christmas.

4 large cooking apples, peeled and
   cored
3 tablespoons demerara sugar
1 tablespoon grated lemon rind
50 g (2 oz) sultanas
375 g (12 oz) Shortcrust Pastry
   (see page 94)
600 ml (1 pint) pale ale
¼ teaspoon grated nutmeg
¼ teaspoon cinnamon
3 cloves
whipped cream, to serve

Stand the apples in a deep, buttered pie dish and then sprinkle them with 2 tablespoons of the sugar and 1 teaspoon of grated lemon peel. Fill the centre of each apple with some sultanas.

Roll out the pastry 1 cm (½ inch) thick on a lightly floured board. Cover the filled apples with the sheet of pastry and then bake in a preheated oven, 200°C (400°F), Gas Mark 6, for 30 minutes.

Put the ale, nutmeg, cinnamon, cloves and the remaining sugar in a small pan and then heat gently over a low heat without boiling.

Carefully loosen the crust and lift the pastry off the apples. Pour the ale mixture over the apples. Cut the pastry into 4 pieces and place one on top of each apple. Serve very hot with some whipped cream.

Serves 4

Cherry Bumpers

375 g (12 oz) cherries, pitted
50 g (2 oz) sugar
1 tablespoon water
250 g (8 oz) Shortcrust Pastry
   (see page 94)
milk, for glazing

Put the cherries, sugar and water in a saucepan. Cook gently over a low heat, stirring occasionally, until the cherries are softened – this takes about 5 minutes. Leave to cool.

Roll out the pastry on a lightly floured board and cut into twelve 10 cm (4 inch) rounds. Divide the cherries between the rounds and dampen the edges of the pastry. Draw up the pastry over the filling, pressing the edges to seal. Flute the join by pinching with the fingers.

Place the bumpers on a baking sheet and brush with a little milk. Bake them in a preheated oven, 200°C (400°F), Gas Mark 6, for 20–25 minutes until golden brown. Serve warm or cold.

Makes 12

left: apple strudel
below: apple Florentine pies

Mince Pies

375 g (12 oz) Rich Shortcrust Pastry
(see page 94)
4–5 tablespoons mincemeat
1 tablespoon brandy
milk, for glazing
sifted icing sugar, for dusting

Roll out half of the pastry fairly thinly on a floured surface and cut out 10–12 rounds, using a 6 cm (2½ inch) fluted cutter. Roll out the other half of the pastry a little thinner than the first and cut out 7.5 cm (3 inch) rounds. Use them to line 10–12 patty tins.

Mix the mincemeat with the brandy and then divide between the patty tins. Dampen the edges of the pastry, place the smaller rounds on top and press the edges together. Make a hole in the centre of each pie and brush with a little milk.

Bake the pies in a preheated oven, 200°C (400°F), Gas Mark 6, for 15–20 minutes until golden brown. Dust with icing sugar and serve warm.

Makes 10–12

Kentish Pudding Pie

This very good pudding was hardly known outside Kent until recent times. However, it is so good that it deserves to be discovered by a wider audience.

900 ml (1½ pints) milk
125 g (4 oz) ground rice
250 g (8 oz) Shortcrust Pastry
(see page 94)
140 g (4½ oz) butter
50 g (2 oz) caster sugar

3 eggs

50 g (2 oz) sultanas, raisins or
    currants

¼ teaspoon freshly grated nutmeg

2 tablespoons double cream

Pour the milk into a saucepan and stir in the ground rice. Bring to the boil, then lower the heat and cook, stirring, for 10 minutes or until the mixture thickens. Remove the pan from the heat and then allow to cool for 15 minutes.

Meanwhile, line a pie dish with the pastry, turning the crust over the edge of the dish and marking it with a fork.

Cream 125 g (4 oz) butter with the sugar until light, fluffy and pale, and then beat in the eggs, one at a time. Stir the mixture into the ground rice and milk, add the dried fruit and nutmeg and beat well. Stir in the cream.

Pour the mixture into the pie dish and then dot the top with the remaining butter.

Bake the pie in the centre of a preheated oven, 180°C (350°F), Gas Mark 4, for 35 minutes. Serve hot or cold with cream or custard.

Serves 4–6

Cumberland Rum Nickies

Rum nickies are traditional cakes in Cumbria and there are various recipes. Some omit the dates and use currants flavoured with nutmeg instead.

125 g (4 oz) dates, pitted and
    chopped

1 tablespoon water

375 g (12 oz) Shortcrust Pastry,
    chilled (see page 94)

3 cooking apples, peeled, cored and
    sliced

1 tablespoon demerara sugar

2 tablespoons rum

50 g (2 oz) butter

milk, for glazing

Butter a 17–20 cm (7–8 inch) pie plate. Put the chopped dates in a saucepan with the water, and cook gently over a low heat to soften them, and then cool completely.

Divide the pastry in half. Roll out one-half and use to line the pie plate. Place the sliced apples on the pastry and scatter the sugar over them. Mix the rum with the butter into the dates and then spread over the apples.

Roll out the remaining pastry for a lid, dampening the edges and pressing them down. Lightly prick all over the top of the pie with a fork, brush lightly with milk and then bake in a preheated oven, 200°C (400°F), Gas Mark 6, for 15 minutes, then reduce the oven temperature to 180°C (350°F), Gas Mark 4, and continue cooking for a further 15 minutes or until the top is golden brown. Serve hot or cold, cut into wedges, with some lightly whipped cream.

Serves 6

left: mince pies
right: Cumberland rum nickies

Basic Recipes

Shortcrust Pastry

250 g (8 oz) plain flour
50 g (2 oz) butter
50 g (2 oz) lard
salt
2–3 tablespoons cold water

Sift the flour and a pinch of salt into a mixing bowl and rub in the fat with the fingertips until the mixture resembles breadcrumbs. Stir in enough water to make a firm dough. Knead lightly until smooth, wrap in clingfilm and chill for 30 minutes. Use as required.

Makes 375 g (12 oz)

Rich Shortcrust Pastry

300 g (10 oz) plain flour
175 g (6 oz) butter
1 egg yolk, beaten with 1 tablespoon cold water

Sift the flour into a bowl and rub in the butter with the fingertips until the mixture resembles breadcrumbs. Stir in enough beaten egg yolk to make a firm dough. Wrap in clingfilm and chill for 30 minutes. Use as required.

Makes 500 g (1 lb)

Short Flan Pastry

1 egg
150 g (5 oz) butter, softened
250 g (8 oz) plain flour, sifted
salt

Whisk the egg and a pinch of salt together, then mix into the butter, a little at a time. Add the flour and mix to a firm dough. Knead lightly until smooth, wrap in clingfilm and chill for 30 minutes. Use as required.

Makes 400 g (14 oz)

Crispy Butter Pastry

250 g (8 oz) plain flour
150 g (5 oz) butter, chilled
salt
3 tablespoons iced water

Sift the flour and a pinch of salt into a bowl. Rub in the butter with the fingertips until the mixture resembles breadcrumbs. Stir in enough water to make a firm dough. Knead lightly until smooth. Wrap in clingfilm and chill for 30 minutes. Use as required.

Makes 400 g (14 oz)

Easy Flaky Pastry

Everything for this recipe must be cold so that the butter is distributed in tiny particles throughout the pastry.

375 g (12 oz) plain flour
50 g (2 oz) lard, chilled
175 g (6 oz) butter, chilled and cut into 5 mm (¼ inch) dice
salt
6 tablespoons iced water

Sift the flour and a pinch of salt into a bowl and rub in the lard with the fingertips. Add the diced butter and rub in until the mixture resembles breadcrumbs. Sprinkle on the water and mix with a knife to a smooth dough. Turn onto a floured surface and shape into a flat disc. Wrap in clingfilm and chill for 1 hour. Use as required.

Makes 625 g (1¼ lb)

Wholemeal Shortcrust Pastry

175 g (6 oz) wholemeal flour
75 g (3 oz) butter or margarine
salt
2–3 tablespoons cold water

Put the flour and a pinch of salt in a mixing bowl and rub in the fat with the fingertips until the mixture resembles breadcrumbs. Add enough water to mix to a firm dough. Knead lightly, then wrap in clingfilm and chill for 30 minutes. Use as required.

Makes 275 g (9 oz)

Cheese Shortcrust Pastry

175 g (6 oz) plain flour
75 g (3 oz) butter or margarine
50 g (2 oz) mature Cheddar cheese, grated
pinch of cayenne pepper (optional)
salt and pepper
2–3 tablespoons cold water

Sift the flour into a bowl and rub in the fat with the fingertips until the mixture resembles breadcrumbs. Stir

in the grated cheese, cayenne (if using) and salt and pepper. Add enough cold water to mix to a firm dough. Knead lightly, then wrap in clingfilm and chill for 30 minutes. Use as required.

Makes 325 g (11 oz)

White Sauce

25 g (1 oz) butter
25 g (1 oz) plain flour
300 ml (½ pint) milk
pinch of nutmeg (optional)
salt and pepper

Melt the butter in a small pan and stir in the flour. Cook gently over a low heat for 2 minutes, stirring, and then gradually beat in the milk, a little at a time. Blend thoroughly between each addition. Bring to the boil, then reduce the heat and simmer gently for 3–4 minutes.

Season with nutmeg (if using) and salt and pepper.

Makes 300 ml (½ pint)

Pâte Sucrée

250 g (8 oz) plain flour
125 g (4 oz) butter, softened
125 g (4 oz) caster sugar
4 egg yolks
few drops of vanilla essence

Sift the flour onto a working surface, make a well in the centre and place the butter, sugar, egg yolks and vanilla in the well. Using the fingertips of one hand, work these ingredients together until well blended, then draw into the flour. Knead lightly until smooth and chill for 1 hour. Use as required.

Makes 500 mg (1 lb)

Index